Stock Market 101: 3 Hour Crash Course

Investing for beginners

Edward Day

from various sources. Please consult a licensed professional before attempting any techniques outlined in this book.

By reading this document, the reader agrees that under no circumstances is the author responsible for any losses, direct or indirect, that are incurred as a result of the use of the information contained within this document, including, but not limited to, errors, omissions, or inaccuracies.

Table of Contents

"Everyone has the power to follow the stock market. If you made it through fifth grade math, you can do it."

— *Peter Lynch*

Introduction

Why should you include stocks in your financial portfolio? To make money, of course. That's the biggest reason why people get involved in the stock market, and it's probably why you've chosen this book. There's no shame in wanting to make your money work harder for you, and it certainly won't do that if it's lazing around in a savings account (in fact, if you take inflation into account you actually lose money if you allow it to stagnate in a bank account instead of investing it).

There are 18.6 million millionaires (and 607 billionaires) in the United States of America, and there's really not anything stopping you from joining their ranks. In fact, a study which was published in 2017 found that over 80% of millionaires are self-made (and very many of them acquired a large portion of this wealth through the stock market). This means that you can multiply your wealth too you're willing to devote some time to learning the ins and outs of stock trading — or, you could invest a little less and happily earn a decent side income. Studies have shown that you should get a minimum average return of 7% - 10% on the money you've invested in the stock market (though obviously your earning potential would actually be much, much higher). Regardless of which of these two you're planning to pursue, you'll need to know the basics of stock trading in order to be successful. Fortunately, we'll cover all of the bases together, and by the end of chapter six, you'll be well on your way to being the next Warren Buffett.

A taste of success in the stock market led me to change careers entirely, but I'm no stranger to how daunting all of the lingo, terminology, and formulae can be to a beginner. I'm 46 now, but I was about 34 when I quit my job as an accountant to become a full-time forex trader (forex traders trade in currency — buying currency from one country and converting it to the currency of another in order to make a profit). I spent a large portion of my life studying to be an accountant. I completed a bachelor's degree in finance, followed by a master's degree in accounting, but I knew that my potential was being wasted as an accountant. I bet you're feeling the same way, and you're probably not wrong.

I had a mentor too, just like I'm going to mentor you. He was a client who I did some work for as an accountant. One day he invited me along to a seminar on forex trading, I was hooked and a new friendship was born from it. I knew that I wanted to know everything there was to know about finance, the economy, and how they tied into the stock market, so off I went and completed another degree (this time a bachelor's in economics) and a myriad of courses in forex trading. Within no time, I was being invited to give talks at finance courses on forex trading, and I was mentoring students of my own. Passing on the knowledge I've acquired is incredibly important to me because I feel that I need to 'pay it forward' out of gratitude to my own personal friend and mentor.

We're not all that different, you and I. I enjoy fishing in my spare time, and I'm on cloud nine when I'm walking my dogs, I'm just a normal guy. This means that, regardless of how average you believe yourself to be, you're capable of achieving everything I have. When I look at my amazing wife and two beautiful daughters, I know that it was all worth it, and it'll be worth it for you too.

I'm not the only average guy to have made it big through the power of the stock market. Ray Dalio did too. At the moment Ray's net worth is $18.7 billion (you would have to earn $200 000 every month for 7791 years in order to make $18.7 billion — it's a lot of money), but it all started off with a stock that he bought at the tender age of 12. It was the early 1960s, and Ray was working as a caddy at a golf course earning about $6 per bag. He saved up until he had $300 (which amounted to about 50 bags' worth of caddying) and spent it all on shares in Northeast Airlines (which became Delta Airlines in later years). At the time, shares in this company were selling for less than $5 per share, which is exactly why Ray decided to buy them. In recent interviews, Ray has urged other young investors not to buy stocks simply because they're cheap, but it was a move that worked for him. Shortly after purchasing shares in Northeast Airlines, the company was bought by Howard Hughes and the price of its shares skyrocketed. Ray kept building his portfolio by buying more and more stocks with money he made from mowing lawns, delivering newspapers, and caddying. By the time he graduated from high school, he owned thousands of dollars' worth of shares. If Ray could finance his eventual success with a caddy's wages, you can do it with whatever amount you'd like to invest too. Your success in the stock market won't be determined by the amount of money you throw at it, but by your strategy.

Ray isn't the only millionaire who made it big in the stock market as a youngster. Tim Sykes, whose current net worth is $15 million, started off by investing $12,000 (which he got as a bar mitzvah present from his parents) in penny stocks. Within two years, that $12,000 had grown to $800,000. Tim was a full-blown millionaire by the age of 21, and was soon running his own hedge fund (a hedge fund is a company which pools the capital of investors and manages it in order to purchase a broad set of stocks, ranging from long term to short term, which charges a percentage of the investors' net assets and profits).

There's another 'Tim' who got rich off of penny stocks at a young age — Tim Grittani (whose net worth is about $6 million). Grittani always knew he wanted to make money (a lot of it), so he investigated every possible avenue of revenue and soon found himself addicted to gambling (while still at college). After losing all of his money in an unfortunate series of bad bets, he realized that it wasn't a sustainable way of making money and quit. At some point someone has probably told you that the stock market is a gamble — that's not entirely true, as Grittani himself proved. In fact, studies show that the stock market has continued its upward trajectory over the past 100 years due to the global economies' sustained growth. Within a year of getting involved in the stock market (and buying up thousands of penny stocks), he had managed to turn the $1,500 which he had initially invested into $128,000. Within 36 months, Grittani had managed to turn it into $1 million.

It's not just a man's world though. Anne Scheiber is heralded a stock market heroine. She lived in the early 1940s and spent her life working as an auditor for the American Internal Revenue Service. Anne retired at 51 with a retirement portfolio of about $297,000 (adjusted for inflation). Anne never had any children, lived in the same tiny apartment all of her life, and never married, which means that she was able to save about four-fifths of her total income. Anne would live to be 101 which means that she was tasked with making this $297,000 last for 50 years, and she managed to do so by investing most of it in the stock market. At the time of her death in 1995, Anne's portfolio was worth about $36 million. Anne managed to increase her portfolio's size by 121 times by steadily buying up more and more dividend-paying stocks over the years, often reinvesting her profits in more stocks. Upon her death, she donated her entire estate to Yeshiva University in order to create a scholarship for Jewish female students.

If Anne, Ray and the two Tims can do it — so can you, and as you've read, you don't need a massive initial investment in order to be successful. Hundreds (if not thousands) of millionaires started with absolutely nothing to their names, and built their wealth by investing every spare penny they earned (and investing it wisely).

Chapter 1:

What is The Stock Market, and Why is It Important?

The "stock market" isn't corporeal, and it isn't just one singular thing — instead "stock market" is the collective term for all of the marketplaces (like the New York Stock Exchange or Chicago Board Options Exchange) where shares and securities are publicly traded.

It's also the most reliable indicator of a country's economic well-being. Countries whose stock exchanges show constant upward growth generally also show a gradual increase in gross domestic product (GDP).

The stock market's purpose is to help companies to raise capital, but smart investors are able to make use of it in order to increase their own profits too. The stock market is incredibly 'liquid' which means that stocks are easy to buy and sell (especially when compared to other investments like real estate which can take months to buy or sell).

The biggest barrier keeping your average Joe from accessing the stock market is a miniscule knowledge deficit. People feel that they don't know enough about the stock market, so they never buy shares, so they never feel like they need to learn about the stock market, and this ugly cycle just keeps repeating itself *ad nauseam* — it's the reason why many people feel the stock market is inaccessible.

Luckily for you, we're going to start bridging that knowledge deficit in this chapter. Keep your chin up, you'll feel well-acquainted with this new world of investing in no time.

Getting to Know the Lingo

There's no point in going any further until I cover some important terms pertaining to stock trading. The stock market has a language all its own, and it's something you'll need to be fluent in in order to truly feel that you've started down the road to mastery of it. Commit these terms to memory, and you'll be speaking 'trader' fluently with ease:

12b-1 Fees: This is a fee you pay to a mutual fund (which is defined below) as one of the requirements of being a member. The money from it typically goes to paying the salespeople in the mutual fund's commissions.

All or none order (AON): This an order you give your broker which he or she is only allowed to execute if he or she can execute it in full. An example of this would be if you told your broker to buy 100 shares in Apple before the end of the trading day under an all or none order — if there were only 90 Apple shares available for sale during the trading day, your broker would buy none of them because he or she would have been unable to fulfill your order of 100 shares in Apple.

Alpha: A stock's alpha number represents whether or not it is outperforming the market in general. Alpha numbers usually represent the percentage by which a certain stock has outperformed, or underperformed, when compared to the rest of the market (a stock that has an alpha number of +3 usually means that it has outdone the rest of the stocks in that market by 3%, while a stock with an alpha number of -3 has probably experienced 3% less growth than the market average).

American depository receipts (ADR): ADRs are receipts that are issued to investors upon purchasing a foreign stock through an American stock exchange. ADRs trade as shares themselves.

Annual report: An annual report is a document that companies are obligated to supply their shareholders with every year. This document should contain information about the company's financial and operating conditions, financial statements (like income statements, cash flow statements and balance sheets), and an auditor's report (amongst others). You'll use an annual report as part of your research into whether a company has the potential for further growth (and thus whether you should invest in its shares). Most companies have their annual reports uploaded to their websites, making them incredibly easy to find for potential investors.

Arbitrage: This is an investment strategy that involves buying shares at one price through one marketplace or exchange, and selling it at a higher market price through another. For example, you might buy a share through the New York Stock Exchange (NYSE) for $5, and then sell it again through The Nasdaq for $5.50.

Ask: The minimum amount of money that a seller is willing to accept for a particular share.

At the money: A stock is said to be 'at the money' when it's trading at the price that you were planning to sell it at.

Authorized stock: This refers to the total number of shares that a company is allowed to issue. This number is always higher than the number of shares available for sale to the public as various role-players within the company will own large numbers of shares too.

Averaging down: Averaging down is an investment technique that you might use when you're buying a long term stock. If you already owned 10 shares that you had purchased at $5 per share, and you saw the shares' prices suddenly dropping to $4, averaging down would be if you went ahead and bought another 10 shares in the same company, paying less for the shares this time around and thus driving down the average amount that you paid per share as you now own 20 shares purchased at an average price of $4.50, instead of 10 shares purchased at $5 (which means that you'll increase your growth ratio on paper when the market picks up again and the shares' regain their original price).

Back-end load: This is a 'penalty' that you have to pay when selling shares in a mutual fund. It is usually calculated by taking a percentage of the total value of the stocks which the fund owns.

Bear market: When the stock market takes a dip and shares start decreasing in value, traders refer to this time period as a 'bear market.' It's a good idea to buy stocks during a bear market so that you can profit off of their sale when the stock market recovers and the shares regain their value.

Bear raid: This is when shareholders of a particular stock sell their shares *en masse* very cheaply in order to drive down the stock's value.

Beta: Beta is a number assigned to companies to help investors determine how risky investing in them would be. Markets have a beta of 1. Companies who show more growth than the market average have a beta of more than 1, while companies who show less growth than the market average have a beta of less than one. Thus, if you're purchasing shares from a company with a beta above 1, you can be relatively sure that those shares will continue to increase in value over time.

Bid: Your bid is the maximum amount of money you're willing to pay for a particular share.

Bid-ask spread: The bid-ask spread is the difference between what you're willing to pay for a stock, and what you can sell it for. You can use a company's bid-ask spread to determine how risky investing in it would be. Companies with a small bid-ask spread are generally low-risk, while companies with a large bid-ask spread are generally high risk. A company like Apple has a small bid-ask spread, you might pay $247.50 dollars for a share in Apple, and you'll probably only be able to sell it for $247.70.

Block trade: A block trade is when you buy a large number of shares (as in, 10,000 or more) all at once.

Blue chip stocks: If you're buying shares in Apple, you're buying blue chip stocks. Blue chip stocks are shares of large (usually multinational) companies that have been performing well for years. Buying blue chip stocks isn't a gamble, and you're basically guaranteed returns, but your potential profit is also reduced by the stability of the stock itself (you'll probably always be able to sell them for a lot of money, but you'll have to buy them for a lot of money too).

Bourse: Bourse is just another word for 'stock market,' though if you hear a trader mentioning it they're probably specifically referring to the Paris Stock Exchange (PAR). There's no particular reason for this, it's just the way language evolved over time. Bourse originally referred to all stock markets because the word itself originated as a bastardization of 'Van Der Burse'. The Van Der Burse House used to be a place in Belgium during the 1500s where merchants would gather to buy and sell goods.

Broker (or stockbroker): A broker is someone who manages your stock portfolio. You give them the order to buy or sell stocks, and they do it for you. It might seem silly to use a broker, but it makes sense when you think about the fact that you can't trade on exchanges like Nasdaq and NYSE if you're not a member (or employed by a member firm). Brokers save you the hassle of having to become a member in order to participate in the stock market.

Bull market: A bull market is the opposite of a bear market (which was defined just above). It's the name given to a period of time in which the stock market experiences an upswing and share prices increase. Selling your shares in a bull market helps you to maximize your profits.

Buyback: Sometimes companies are willing to reacquire the shares which they previously made available to the public through an initial private offering or second offering. This is called a 'buyback' or a 'buyback scheme'.

Buying on margin: This is another term for 'leverage' (which is described below), it basically means buying stock with borrowed money.

Capital gain: Capital gain is the difference between what you paid for a stock and what you sold it for. Thus, if you purchased a share for $50 and sold it a year later for $80, your capital gain would be $30.

Capital gains distribution: This is when an exchange-traded fund or mutual fund (both of which are defined below) pays out a percentage of the proceeds which it has made from dividends or from selling stock held within the fund to the traders who have invested in it.

Close: Close is the term used to refer to the time at which a particular stock exchange closes for trading for the day. Nasdaq and the NYSE 'close' at 4 pm Eastern Standard Time (EST), although in recent years after-hours trading has been extended to 8 pm EST. The following stock exchanges close at these times (according to EST):

The Australian Securities Exchange (ASX) - 1 am.
The Hong Kong Stock Exchange (HKEX) - 4 am.
The Irish Stock Exchange (ISE) - 12:30 pm.
The London Stock Exchange (LSE) - 12:30 pm.
The Mexican Stock Exchange (BMV) - 5 pm.
The National Stock Exchange of India (NSE) - 6 am.
The Shanghai Stock Exchange (SSE) - 3 am.
The Tokyo Stock Exchange (TSE) - 2 am.
The Toronto Stock Exchange (TSX) - 4 pm.

Day order: This is an order you give your broker to buy or sell stocks if they reach certain price points during a specified day. This order is only valid during the day which was agreed upon when the order was placed, and expires after this period (which means that if you don't give your broker new instructions or they aren't instructed on what to do after the expiration of this order, they will stop actively trading that stock at the end of the specified day).

Day trading: Day traders (also known as active traders) buy a stock, and sell it on the same day. This fast sale cycle is called day trading. In order to successfully day trade, you need to be able to spot stocks that are going to increase in value within a matter of hours. This strategy is usually only practiced in forex and the stock markets.

Dead cat bounce: This is a term used to refer to when a stock that has rapidly been declining in value, suddenly recovers and starts increasing in value again (giving investors the impression that it is going to start experiencing an upswing), before continuing with its downward trajectory and further decreasing in value.

Diversification: This is when you invest in stocks from a number of different sectors so that if one sector experiences a depression, you'll still have a source of income from the remaining sectors (for example, you would be 'diversifying' your portfolio if you owned shares in Apple, a technology company, and Anglo-American, a mining company).

Dividend: There are two kinds of dividends — cash dividends and stock dividends. A cash dividend is a sum of money (usually calculated per share owned) that is paid out to owners of the company's stock at regular intervals (normally quarterly, semi-annually, annually, or monthly). Stock dividends are like cash dividends, except the company rewards its shareholders with more shares (the amount of shares awarded ordinarily depends on the number of shares already owned by the shareholder). Not all companies who sell their shares offer dividends as they're not obligated to. You should also only be concerned about dividends if the stock is a long term stock.

Dividend aristocrat index: This is a list of large companies which sell blue chip stocks that are named in the Standard and Poor 500 index which have steadily been increasing their dividend payouts over the past quarter of a century (in other words, they're likely to be a good investment).

Exchange traded fund (ETF): An exchange traded fund is a service offered by some brokers which allows you to buy 'bundles' of certain stocks. ETFs are a bit like mutual funds (which are defined below) in the sense that investors' money gets 'pooled' and this pool is managed by the fund's manager. Unlike mutual funds, you can buy 'shares' in an ETF (in fact, they trade as stocks on the various exchanges).

Fifty-two week high: This is a term used to refer to the highest price which a stock sold for over a one year period.

Fifty-two week low: This is a term used to refer to the lowest price which a stock sold for over a one year period.

Fill or kill (FOK) order: If you give your stockbroker a fill or kill order, it means that he or she needs to either execute the order in its entirety or not at all. An example of this would be if you told your stockbroker to buy 100 shares in Apple at $240 a share on a FOK order, if there were only 99 shares available for sale, or there were not 100 shares available at $240 a share, he or she would buy none.

Front-end load: This is a sales fee that you have to pay when you first invest in a mutual fund.

Futures contract: A futures contract is a written agreement between two parties in which the one party binds him- or herself to buying stocks from the other at a later predetermined date for a set predetermined price.

Gap down stocks: A gap down stock is a stock that opens at a lower price than it was trading for at the previous day's close. This happens to stocks whose values are driven down during after-hours trading. When this happens, it's usually indicative of a high-risk stock or stock going through a high-risk period.

Gap up stocks: A gap up stock is a stock that opens at a higher price than it was trading for at the previous day's close (so it's essentially the opposite of a gap down stock). This happens to stocks whose values are driven up during after-hours trading. This occurrence indicates that the affected stock is likely to experience a further upswing during the trading day.

Good-till-cancelled (GTC) orders: This is a type of order that you give your broker instructing him to buy or sell stocks if they reach certain price points during a certain period of time (anything from one to three months is the norm). Once the time period that you've agreed to in the order expires, the order to execute expires too, and the broker will thus stop actively trading that stock until he or she receives new orders.

Growth stock: Growth stock are shares that increase in value (capitalization) over time. They're attractive because of this capital appreciation, but they don't pay investors dividends.

Haircut: This term refers to the difference between what you paid for a stock, and what the bank is willing to consider it's worth as collateral for a loan. If the bank gives you a 30% haircut on shares being used as collateral that you purchased for $100, that means that the bank only recognizes those shares as being worth $70. However, a 'haircut' has a second meaning in traders' lingo, sometimes when traders use this term, they're referring to a small bid-ask spread as described above.

Hedging: To attempt to reduce the risk of an investment.

Hedge fund: Hedge funds are highly unregulated private partnerships representing private investments. Their only goal is to generate a high rate of returns for their investors. Investors 'pool' their money into hedge funds, and the hedge fund's manager uses it to buy and sell stocks in order to generate revenue for these investors. Hedge funds are only available to accredited investors, but generally offer higher returns than mutual funds (which will be defined below).

High: When a stock hits a 'record high', it means that its shares are trading for more than they ever have before. A stock's daily high (or 'today's high') refers to the highest price which a stock traded at before the exchange's close on that day.

Income stock: This is a term used to describe shares that pay out steadily increasing dividends on a regular basis.

Index: An index statistically measures the value of a batch of stocks. This batch of stocks usually represents a certain area of the market, and thus they allow investors to track the growth of certain sectors without having to research each and every stock in them. An index fund invests in these specific sectors on behalf of investors. Examples of index funds are; the Dow Jones Industrial Average (that's 'sector' or 'batch' consists of shares from the 30 biggest American companies) and the Vanguard 500 Index Fund (that's 'sector' consists of hundreds of shares listed on Standard and Poor 500 index).

Index fund: An index fund 'pools' the money of the people who invest in it in order to buy stocks that mirror those listed on well-known indices like the Standard and Poor 500 and the Vanguard 500 Index Fund).

Initial public offering: An initial public offering (IPO) occurs when a private company starts trading publicly. This term refers to the first shares in such a company that are offered for sale through a marketplace like

Nasdaq or the NYSE to any investor that has the money to buy them.

Leverage: There are two different types of 'leverage' that you may encounter during your journey into stock exchange success. The first kind is when you borrow money (either from the bank or from a broker) in order to buy more shares than you would ordinarily be able to afford in the hope of drastically increasing your returns. The second involves borrowing actual shares from a broker with the goal of selling them for more than they were worth when you borrowed them (you would then be able to keep any profits, but would need to pay a fee to the broker and return the stocks to him or her). Both types of leverage are best avoided by beginners because they're a *fantastic* way to lose money if you're not entirely sure about the stock's potential for growth.

Limit move: If you buy a stock for the highest or lowest price which it has traded at during that trading day, you're making a 'limit move'.

Limit order: A limit order is an order you give your broker instructing him or her to sell your stocks should their value increase above a certain point, or to buy new stocks should their value decrease below a certain point.

Locked in: You're locked in if taxes, regulations, or your position in a company prevent you from being able to sell certain stocks in your portfolio.

Long position: If you're 'holding a long position' or 'going long' it means that you're buying a stock with the belief that it will increase in value over time.

Low: A 'record low' refers to the lowest price which a stock has ever traded at. A 'daily low' (or 'today's low') refers to the lowest price a stock was sold at before the exchange's close.

Margin: This term relates to leverage (which is described above). It is the difference between the value of the stocks you currently own and the amount of money that you borrowed from the bank or a broker.

Market capitalization: This refers to the dollar value of the shares which a company has for sale. For example, if a company has 1000 shares available for purchase at $5 per share, it has a market capitalization of $5000 dollars. The size of a company directly correlates with the size of its market capitalization. Large companies have market capitalizations of more than $10 billion, medium-sized companies have market capitalizations of more than $2 billion, and small companies have market capitalizations of up to $2 billion. Large companies are usually safe to invest in because their size indicates a predictable rate of profitability.

Market order: A market order is an order that you give your broker to buy or sell stocks immediately at their current market price.

Margin account: A margin account is almost like an overdraft. It's a financial service offered by most brokerage firms that allows you to buy stocks which are worth more than the money you have in your standard account (of course it's only a loan, and this money needs to be paid back).

Moving average: This term refers to the average price of a stock over a specific length of time (usually ranging from the length of a workweek to six months).

Mutual fund: A mutual fund is a publicly offered financial service that allows investors to pool their money together. Much like with hedge funds, mutual fund managers manage this money by buying and selling stocks in whichever way he or she believes will offer the highest rate of return for his or her investors. Unlike with hedge funds, mutual funds are highly regulated by The Securities and Exchange Commission (SEC), specifically through the Investment Company Act of 1940 and the Securities Act of 1933. Unlike hedge funds, you don't need to be an accredited investor in order to be able to buy into a mutual fund.

No-load fund: This term refers to a mutual fund that doesn't charge any sales commissions when you're purchasing stock in it, and doesn't charge any penalties when you're selling stock in it.

Offloading: The act of selling stocks held within one's portfolio.

Open: Open refers to when a stock exchange resumes trading after close. The NYSE and Nasdaq 'open' at 9:30 am EST. Of course, you can still buy shares before these stock exchanges open through premarket trading which commences at 4 am EST. The following stock exchanges open at these times (according to EST):

The Australian Securities Exchange (ASX) - 7 pm.
The Hong Kong Stock Exchange (HKEX) - 9:30 pm.
The Irish Stock Exchange (ISE) - 4 am.
The London Stock Exchange (LSE) - 4 am.
The Mexican Stock Exchange (BMV) - 10:30am.
The National Stock Exchange of India (NSE) - 11:45 pm.
The Shanghai Stock Exchange (SSE) - 9:30 pm.
The Tokyo Stock Exchange (TSE) - 8 pm.
The Toronto Stock Exchange (TSX) - 9:30 am.

Pattern day trader rule - Day traders are traders who buy stocks at the beginning of a trading day, only to sell all of them again before its close. The pattern day trader rule was set by the Financial Industry Regulatory Authority and states that traders need to maintain a minimum account balance of $25,000 if they 'day trade' three or more stocks over a five day period.

Penny stocks: These are 'cheap' stocks that trade for less than five dollars. They aren't sold on any of the major stock exchanges like the NYSE or Nasdaq, instead, they're traded 'over-the-counter' (OTC) — which is why they're sometimes called OTC stocks. This means that if you want to buy them, you would need to do it through a broker-dealer network like the company 'Pink Sheet' or the Over-The-Counter Bulletin Board (OTCBB). These are deemed to be high-risk stocks, so you should think twice before investing in them as a beginner.

Pink sheet stocks: Pink sheet stocks are the same as penny stocks.

Portfolio: Your 'portfolio' is the collective name for all of the stocks that you own.

Program trading: Program trading is when traders who buy and sell stocks online exploit the stocks' price differences across the different online trading platforms by buying or selling large amounts of them for the most favorable price.

Public float: This refers to a company's shares that are owned by private investors or are available for purchase by private investors (so it's the total number of the company's shares subtracted by the 'locked-in' shares which are not available to the public).

Pump and dump: A 'pump and dump' is when investors, executives, or analysts make untrue statements to the media in order to drive up a stock's price, just to offload all of their shares in the company as the price increases.

Put option: A put option is something you can buy from a broker which sets your stock's sale price for a particular period of time. You would buy a put option if you were worried that the stock's price was about to drastically drop but still wanted to be able to sell it at its current price in the future. Imagine you bought 100 shares for $50 per share, but you were concerned that their price could drop to $30 a share within a couple of days, you might purchase a 'put' at $1 per share from your broker in order to 'freeze' the shares' prices at $50 per share. This means you would pay your broker $100 to be able to sell your shares for $5,000, even in the case that they devalue to $3,000 during the agreed time period.

Quote: A quote tells you the price of a stock in a particular stock exchange. It should also tell you the stock's bid price, ask price, the volume of the stock that has been traded, and the last price that the stock traded at. You should carefully review quotes to try and extrapolate whether or not the stock that you've been quoted on has the potential for further growth.

Rally: A rally occurs when stocks suddenly experience a drastic upswing in price caused by increased demand in the stock market.

Risk-reward ratio: A stock's risk-reward ratio indicates the amount of profit a trader can expect to make for every dollar he or she is willing to risk on it. A stock with a 1:5 risk-reward ratio indicates that investors can expect to make $5 for every $1 they spend on that particular stock. If you were to buy 10 stocks at $8 per stock, and decided you would definitely sell them if the stock declined to $6 per stock (which means you are risking losing $20), but you expect the stock to sell at $10 if all goes well (in which case you would make a profit of $20) the risk-reward ratio would be $20:$20 which is 1:1.

Secondary offering: A secondary offering is when a company that has already made an initial public offer offers up more (previously unavailable) shares to the public. A dilutive secondary offering is when the company 'creates' new shares and sells them to the public, a non-dilutive secondary offering is when major stockholders in a company sell off some of their previously held shares to the general public.

Shares: These are 'pieces' of companies that you can buy in the stock market. Owning enough of them can gain you voting rights to issues pertaining to the company's finances and operations.

Share buy back program: A shares buy back program is when a company offers to buy back shares that were issued during its initial public offering. Stocks' prices surge when companies announce a share buy back option, which means that it's almost always good news for investors.

Short-position: A short position is when you sell some of your shares in the hope that their price will decrease later so that you can buy them back at this lower price. If you sell your stocks for $14 per share, and rebuy them for $12 per share, you make a profit of $2 per share.

Short-selling: Short-selling is an investment strategy best left to professionals. It involves borrowing stock from a broker that you believe is going to drastically decrease in value before you have to pay the broker back, and then selling the stock before it experiences this expected decline in value. If this strategy is successful, you'll end up paying the broker less than you made from selling the stocks because of their decrease in value before payment was due.

Simple moving average: This is a way of measuring a stock's moving average. It is calculated by taking the sum of stock's price at the stock exchange's close on each day of the period being considered, and dividing it by the number of days being sampled. For example, if you decided to work out a moving average over five days (a workweek) and the stock's prices at closer were $10, $12, $14, $16, and $18 respectively, then the simple moving average would be $14. The formula would look something like this:

$$\frac{\$10 + \$12 + \$14 + \$16 + \$18}{5 \; days} = \frac{\$70}{5 \; days} =$$ a simple moving average of $14.

Special dividends: These are monetary rewards that dividend-paying companies may pay their shareholders above and beyond regular dividend payments.

Stocks: 'Stocks' is a different name for shares (which are defined above). Stocks and shares are synonymous.

Stock and Poor 500 Index: This is essentially a list of the 500 top-performing companies on American stock markets with market capitalizations (which are defined above) of more than $5 billion. It is more commonly called the S&P 500.

Stock symbol: A stock's symbol consists of one to four letters that have been assigned to represent it in the stock market. Microsoft is MSFT, Apple is AAPL, Amazon is AMZN, Tesla is TSLA, and Mcdonalds is MCD.

Trading volume: This is the number of shares sold in a particular stock over a set period of time (usually one trading day).

Trading day: The trading day starts at the stock exchange's open, and ends at its close.

Value stocks: Value stocks don't drastically increase in value (they don't offer any promising capital appreciation), but they offer high dividends.

Widow-and-orphan stock: This kind of stock is low risk but offers regular payouts of high dividends. They're usually sold by blue chip companies.

The History of the Stock Market

Rome wasn't built in a day, and neither was the stock market.

Although trading government securities has been popular amongst those looking to invest since the twelfth century, the selling of shares by a publicly-traded company didn't happen until the early 1600s.

The stock market didn't come into existence through the spirit of low-risk investing either, instead, it was created for the sole purpose of funding ventures that were too risky for a singular investor to undertake.

In about 1602 the Dutch East India Company created the Amsterdam Stock Exchange (the first in the world) in order to offer 'shares' in its voyages to the general public. Those that bought a 'share' (or shares) in a voyage would be entitled to a corresponding percentage of that voyage's profits (if the voyage was successful). This means that these 'publicly-traded' voyages constituted the first limited liability companies, with each voyage creating a new limited liability company. The Dutch East India Company started offering shares in their voyages to the public in hope of offsetting their losses, as their ships were regularly being seized by Barbary pirates while out on the open seas.

For about 100 years, the Amsterdam Stock Exchange was the only stock exchange which was fully operational, and most of what was traded were shares in voyages (and shares in the company itself in later years).

The Paris Stock Exchange was founded in 1724, and only ever paused its operations (and only for a month) in 1793, during the turmoil and chaos of the French revolution (which saw the beheading of the French monarchy and much of its nobility). With the exception of this disruption, it operated without any hiccups for hundreds of years until its dissolution in 2000.

In the 1600s, the English monarchy started issuing 'shares' in order to fund its many wars. It essentially loaned sums of money from willing English citizens with the promise of repaying them with interest. These 'shares' were so popular amongst the English that the Bank of England was born to oversee them.

Soon the English had decided to give the Dutch's methods a try. The monarchy set up the South Seas Charter (SSC) and immediately started selling thousands of shares in its future voyages. The London Stock Exchange (LSE) was founded by a group of investors in 1773 with the sole purpose of facilitating the trade of stocks like those issued by the SSC.

For a few decades, the English stock market boomed until the (SSC) could no longer pay dividends to its investors because of its lavish spending of the influx in its capital on upgrading its already-overdone offices in London. The general public was so upset by this swindling that the monarchy was forced to ban stock trading in the kingdom of Britain. This ban lasted until 1825.

Nineteen years after the formation of the LSE, 24 American stockbrokers signed the Buttonwood Agreement. By signing this, the stockbrokers agreed to cut out the auctioneers who had previously sold stocks and set their commission fees at 0.25%.

In 1817 these 24 brokers formed the New York Stock and Exchange Board, setting up proper structures of governance and creating sets of fair trade and best practice rules for the organization to operate under. This organization soon became known as the New York Stock Exchange (NYSE), as it's still known today.

The Brussels Stock Exchange was formed 28 years after the London Stock Exchange after Napoleon himself demanded it be created. Brussels wasn't the only country that embraced stock trading in the 19th century.

In 1861 a group of stockbrokers known as the Association of Brokers met in a masonic hall in Canada and formed the Toronto Stock Exchange (TSX) as it is still known today.

In 1878 Japan's Tokyo Stock Exchange (TSE) was formed under the supervision of the country's finance minister at the time. The TSE operated without any problems or qualms until the outbreak of World War Two, which saw it experience a total shut down. It was reopened in 1949, and has since become one of the largest stock markets in the world.

A number of stock markets have been formed more recently, each adapted in its own way to suit the needs of the modern world.

The Nasdaq (formerly known as the National Association of Securities Dealers Automated Quotations) was the first stock market in the world to trade electronically. It was founded in 1971 by the Financial Industry Regulatory Authority. It was initially unpopular with stockbrokers because its bid-ask spreads were smaller than those offered by more traditional stock markets, which, in turn, decreased the stockbrokers' profit margins, but its accessibility quickly made up for any negative sentiment. By the early 1980s, a third of all stock that was being traded in America was being traded on the Nasdaq. By the early 1990s, this number had soared to cover nearly half of all stock transactions in America.

Euronext was created seven years after the formation of the European Union (EU). It saw the amalgamation of the world's oldest stock exchange, the Amsterdam Stock Exchange, with the Paris Bourse and the Brussels Stock Exchange.

We have been trading and investing in stocks in formalized stock exchanges for more than 400 years. I think 400 years of success speaks for itself.

The History of Stock Market Crashes

Someone once told me that a stock market crash is worse than a divorce. Why? Because you lose half your money but have to keep your wife. Of course, I love my wife and would like to keep all of my money — which is why I've invested some time into studying the ins and outs of historical stock market crashes. While it's good to be able to laugh about them, it's also important to know that they've ruined investors and brokers in the past. They're some of the most disastrous occurrences that can befall a trader.

Over its centuries' long life span the stock market has experienced periods in time where it has devalued to disastrously low levels — this doesn't mean that the stock market is an unreliable investment, but knowing how to spot stock market crashes before they happen can help you to liquidize your shares before being impacted by the market's deflation. The best way to learn how to spot an emerging bear market is to study previous bear markets.

The first stock market crash occurred in 1637 and impacted the Amsterdam Stock Exchange. The Dutch stock market crashed because, after a period of artificial inflation, the price of tulip bulbs drastically plummeted, devaluing trader's investments to the point that they were basically worth nothing. This crash was retrospectively named the 'tulip mania bubble'. The term 'tulip mania' is still used by traders and brokers today to refer to a stock that's price has been inflated above its actual value.

The Dutch East India Company didn't only pioneer the first ever stock exchange, they engineered one of the first major economic crises in the stock market too. After the crash of 1637, the most prolific was that of 1769. During this year, the value of shares in the Dutch East India Company skyrocketed due to their colonization of Bengal. This price increase was short lived as a famine in Bengal coupled with an attack on the company's Bengalese holdings caused the Dutch East India Company's shares' prices to enter a downward spiral. Soon shares in this company were trading for just 45% of what they had previously been trading for. It took the Amsterdam Stock Exchange months to recover.

Of course, American stock markets aren't immune to bear markets and depressions either. The NYSE crashed for the first time in 1901, and took nearly three years to recover. Stocks being traded on the NYSE drastically devalued overnight because investors 'panicked', decided to turn their investments into cash, and sold a large number of their shares. The over-supply of stocks available for sale on the NYSE because of this was the main reason for the rapid devaluation of stocks. Why did investors panic? Well, the President at the time, William McKinley was assassinated in September of 1901, just six months into his first term, causing investors to become concerned for the country's economic well-being. Other driving factors included a fight over the monopolization of the Northern railways, and a severe drought which struck large areas of the country in the final months of the year.

The most devastating American stock market crash of all time occurred on the NYSE in 1929, and is known as 'the Wall Street crash of 1929'. It led to the Great Depression, and was so prolific that the day of the crash received its own name — Black Tuesday (some stockbrokers actually dove out of their high rise office buildings' windows when the crash was announced, such was the financial devastation which it caused). The Wall Street crash of 1929 was preceded by the roaring twenties, a decade which basically set the NYSE up for failure. One of the main reasons for this crash was the over-production of goods by publicly-traded companies. Innovations in production enabled companies to exponentially increase their production, but sales were unable to keep up — which means that companies saw their profit margins drastically decrease despite manufacturing more goods than ever before. This decrease in profitability naturally led to a decrease in the value of production companies' stocks. The economic boom of the 1920s also saw investors becoming overly brash, with more and more of them buying larger and larger quantities of stock on credit or on margin. Shareholders who owned stock which had been purchased with an outstanding loan were the first to dump their shares at below-market prices when the NYSE started declining in 1929 in an attempt to reclaim their money, this further fueled the decline of The NYSE's stocks' prices. The United States of America's Federal Reserve Bank increased interest rates by 6% in the preceding year too, which further caused investors to cut the number of stocks which they owned in order to pay their debts.

The next significant American stock market crash happened in 1987 and is named 'Black Monday'. It earned this moniker because it was the largest stock market devaluation to ever happen within a singular day. The Dow Jones Industrial Average suffered the most, with its stock decreasing in value by 22%. This crash was caused by program trading which caused illiquidity in the stock market (as traders bought up or sold incredibly large numbers of stocks at once). Most stock markets have developed a strategy involving 'circuit breakers' in order to prevent a market crash like this one from ever happening again. These circuit breakers usually mean that a stock market will suspend trading for predetermined periods of time should it devalue below certain percentage points (for example, a stock market might suspend trading for fifteen minutes if it devalues by 7% within one trading day).

Stock markets experienced an upswing in the 1990s as internet companies started trading publicly. Investors went wild for their stocks because they were something new and unknown — investors thought that these companies were the future of commerce. Shares in companies like Google, Amazon, eBay, and Shutterfly were snatched up and their prices were driven up by the surge in demand. Of course, this bubble soon burst, with the early 2000s seeing many stock markets crash as dot-com companies' stocks rapidly devalued as many of them went bankrupt and speculation decreased.

The second worst global financial crisis to ever have occurred (after the Great Depression of 1929) was the financial crisis of 2007 which saw stock markets across the world crash. The cause of this dominating bear market was damage done to the fiscal health of banking institutions in America because of Americans' tendency to default on loans. The crisis started with the global financial institution, Lehman Brothers, declaring bankruptcy (which caused the Dow Jones to drop by hundreds of points). A couple of months after the aforementioned company filed for bankruptcy, Washington Mutual bank followed suit.

The most recent stock market crash happened in early 2020 amidst the COVID-19 outbreak and affected all of the global stock markets. As countries went into lockdown in order to 'flatten the curve' (of infections) and curb the outbreak of the disease, companies that are publicly-traded stocks started to lose their value as they decreased their production and limited their operations. Not only were the companies themselves devaluing their stocks, investors started converting their investments back into cold hard cash in order to protect them, increasing the supply of shares for sale and thus driving their values down even further.

From analyzing these historical stock market crashes, we can extrapolate that they're usually caused by circumstances outside of the realm of stock trading (like political disturbances and natural disasters) or by the artificial inflation of certain stocks beyond what their inherent, intrinsic value actually was.

Why You Should Invest in the Stock Market

Everybody wants to invest in the stock market in order to make money, but not everybody understands how the stock traders generate their income. There are two ways to make money out of shares: dividends and capital appreciation (the increase of a stock's value over time). The money you make from capital appreciation alone should be about five times higher than the current rate of inflation, which means that while goods and services are becoming more and more expensive, money invested in the stock market is growing five times as fast. Comparatively, money placed in a savings account grows by about 0.5% per annum, while investments made in the stock market grow by about 10% every year.

Another reason why people choose to invest in stocks is to diversify their investments (for example, if you've invested in real estate, investing in stocks can ensure that you have a steady income even if the real estate market stagnates).

The Risks of Investing in the Stock Market

As was discussed earlier, stock market crashes are one of the biggest threats to traders' wealth, but they certainly aren't the only concern.

All shares' prices fluctuate over time. These constant fluctuations make it difficult to predict what a stock's price will be at any set point in time (although some traders pride themselves on allegedly being able to do just that). This means that stocks aren't always the best short term investment as a stock you bought today may only be worth half of what you paid for it tomorrow — in fact, stocks are really only a 'safe' investment if you're willing to consider them a long term investment (as you're virtually guaranteed that they'll increase in value over time).

The final risk to consider is the bankruptcy of the company whose shares you own. Most shareholders own ordinary shares, which means that should the company that issued them go bankrupt they'll be last in line to be refunded for their investment. When publicly-traded companies are liquidated, creditors and holders of preferred stock are the first to get paid — this means that if you own ordinary stock, you might not get paid anything for the stock you owned.

Why You Should Invest in American Stock Markets

The American economy in its entirety has become a dominating force — and it's no surprise if you consider that it's the largest economy in the world (in fact, it accounts for 25% of the global gross domestic product. The dollar has become the currency of choice for international transactions, and the United States of

America has become the most important export destination for a fifth of the world's countries.

American stock markets are the world's financial powerhouses. In fact, the American stock market is 500% bigger than its closest competitor, China. Publicly-traded American companies' market capitalization is about $176 trillion. Publicly-traded non-American companies' market capitalization is less than a quarter of that. Without even having to dive any deeper into the numbers, it's already pretty apparent that the American stock market is possibly the most important role player in the global stock trade.

Despite the fact that Americans only make up about 5% of the world's population, 43% of the money which exchanges hands globally because of stock transactions is spent in American stock exchanges (although only 17% of the total volume of stocks traded globally is traded here).

The two biggest stock exchanges within the American stock market are the NYSE and Nasdaq (the former's market capitalization is about $21 trillion, while the latter's market capitalization is $11 trillion). There are 2,400 companies that trade publicly on the NYSE, and 3,800 which do so on the Nasdaq. These two stock exchanges form the backbone of the American stock market.

The pure size of the American stock market should be enough to convince you that it's the stock market for you because its enormity is indicative of its ongoing fiduciary success. Its size isn't the only thing it has going for it though.

The American stock market is also the most expensive stock market in the world (according to a survey conducted by Barclays Bank), which means that the stock prices here are notably higher than in other countries. This can make the initial 'buy in' into the stock market a bit more difficult for Americans, but it also means that American stocks are an ever-appreciating asset.

Some of the biggest and most influential companies in the world trade their stocks on the American stock market, which means that it's the place to be if you're looking to buy high yield stocks.

The Future of the Stock Market

A hundred years ago all of the transactions concluded in all of the stock markets in the world had to be recorded on paper and notarized into a central database, if you wanted to know a stock's price you had to buy the daily paper, and the stage was being set for the Great Depression. Ten years ago, the American stock market was recovering from the 2007 recession which saw $13 trillion worth of trader's stock investments turn to dust.

What will the stock market look like 10 years from now? Analysts have tried to answer this question in order to help traders plan their investments.

One of the main speculations made by analysts is that the American economy's growth is set to decelerate over the next couple of years. Analysts believe that the American economy's growth will be no more than 1.8% per year until about 2029. This is low even when compared to 2019's already-low growth of 2.3%. Analysts also think that America's federal debt will increase to be equal to 93% of the country's GDP by 2029. Both of these factors are likely to lead to company's holding onto any meager profits which they might generate under such trying conditions, leading to the rate of capital appreciation slowing down and a decrease in dividend payments.

Despite this relatively negative outlook for the American economy, analysts from Macquarie Investment Management say that the American stock market will double in value by 2030, and that the high value stocks of that time will belong to health food companies and emerging medical technology companies.

Some economists believe that global warming may increasingly start affecting the stock market over the next couple of years too. Firstly, it's speculated that bear markets will become the norm as climate change increases the prevalence of natural disasters. This downward spiral is likely to be kickstarted by agricultural companies defaulting on their bank loans as their crops become compromised due to extreme weather patterns. The United States' Government Accountability Office itself has stated that it believes that global warming may cost it $112 billion per annum. Some of the extreme weather patterns we've experienced over the past two or three years have already cost a few publicly traded companies millions. The reinsurance firm Munich Re lost about $24 billion dollars due to the wildfires that ravaged California in 2019.

The constant threat of damage resulting from global warming shouldn't put you off of investing in the stock market though. Instead, you should see it as an opportunity to choose your stocks more wisely. A study conducted by the Deutsche Bank found that environmentally-friendly companies' capital appreciation increased by 1.1% more every year than their less environmentally-conscious counterparts. In other words, you should research a company's environmental stance before investing in its shares as it might affect how profitable its shares will be in the long run.

If you're looking to ride the environmentally-friendly wave (and make some money doing it), there are four specific sectors that you should consider investing in: wind energy, water, waste and recycling, and specialized building materials.

If you're looking to buy into the wind energy sector, you should consider buying shares in General Electric (and fortunately, they've only recently started recovering from a three year long downswing, so you should be able to scoop up some shares that won't cost you an arm and a leg). General Electric has had quite an impressive wind energy department for some time, but it proved its commitment to green energy when it started taking over successful wind energy companies and merging them into its own operations in 2016. It would be reasonable to assume that General Electric will continue to follow this trend, which means that its shares are set to increase in value as the world slowly starts decreasing its use of fossil fuels.

Two or three years ago, Denmark's Vestas Wind Systems (Vestas) was trading as an over-the-counter stock, today one of its shares costs more than $80. This European company has a market capitalization of about $18 billion and is the largest manufacturer of wind turbines in the world. Vestas isn't set to slow down any time soon as the company has 36 billion dollars' worth of backlogged orders. Buying shares in Vestas is a brilliant option for investors who have a bit more capital, and who would like to invest in shares that are guaranteed to drastically increase in value over time.

There is a wind energy company that is outperforming even General Electric and Vestas in the stock market: Ørsted (it was called DONG Energy until 2017). At the moment a single share in Ørsted trades for just under $100, and analysts expect its shares to continue increasing in value over the next decade. This company owns both of the worlds' largest offshore wind farms and is the leading energy company in its country of origin, Denmark.

The water sector's shares are arguably even lower risk than the wind energy sector's. Scientists believe that the world's population will reach 10 billion by 2050, which means that we will need to supply more than 2 billion additional people (and the commercial growth that comes with them) with water. Consequently, companies involved in the supply, distribution, or filtration of water are set to experience major economic growth over the next couple of years.

One of the emerging water companies that you should keep an eye on is Sabesp (one of Brazil's water utility companies) which is trading for just under $8 at the moment. Its shares' prices doubled between 2018 and 2019, and there's no reason to believe that they won't continue on this tangent as the demand for water continues to grow in Brazil. Sabesp is a good choice for someone who is looking for shares that regularly pay out high dividends as it has paid out about 20% of its profits over the past year as dividends to its shareholders.

If you're skeptical about investing in an international water company, and you'd prefer something a little closer to home, you should consider investing in the California Water Service Group. Its stocks' values increased by almost a third between 2017 and 2018 due to an increase in its operations. It was forced to increase its operational capacity because of the prevailing drought which affected New Mexico and California at the time. Scientists believe that droughts will become more common as climate change continues to affect the landscape around us, which means that the California Water Service Group's growth is far from over.

The third economic sector that will continue to experience growth because of climate change and the growing population is waste and recycling. The growing population means that companies need to contend with growing volumes of waste, while environmental pressures mean that waste management companies have been forced to innovate how they deal with this increase of waste. One of the companies which has managed to stay ahead of the trend is Waste Management Inc, which supplies waste management services to tens of millions of Canadians, Americans, and Puerto Ricans. All three of the aforementioned nationalities are experiencing sustained growth in their populations, which means that Waste Management Inc. has a steady supply of future customers (and thus a promise for sustained demand of their services). This company has also made an effort to stay relevant by keeping up with its environmental obligations. One of Waste Management Inc.'s landfills started producing thousands of gallons of clean burning fuel in 2009 in order to help fuel a local electric power plant. Shares in this company are a safe bet for investors looking to purchase shares as a long term investment as this company's environmental policies and guaranteed operational growth indicate that it will probably experience immense capital appreciation over the next couple of years.

The final sector which is set to benefit from the climate change craze is specialized building materials. This sector might sound complicated, but it essentially consists of companies that produce or sell adaptive building materials which facilitate the building of environmentally friendly homes and offices. As we strive to lower our energy consumption and shrink our carbon footprints, some companies are cashing in on the change in building styles and materials. If you're looking to buy into this sector, shares in Owens Corning are a good option. Owens Corning specializes in manufacturing thermal insulation for residential and commercial buildings (homes and offices that are properly insulated spend less on heating, which means that they're using less gas or electricity too). This company's shares sell for about $40 per share, which is a bargain for shares in a company that has been on the Fortune 500 for more than 65 years.

It's also believed that the price of gas and crude oils is set to skyrocket over the next decade (which means that investing in shares in oil companies might still be a good idea despite the 'green revolution'). You might want to consider specifically investing in American oil companies, as researchers think that America will start exporting more oil than it imports within the next two or three years.

Investors are often hesitant to invest in shares in technology companies, probably because of the 2000 recession caused by the dot-com bubble, but there's no better time to scoop up their shares than now. The past year saw shares in technology companies greatly outperform those from other sectors — in fact, technology companies offered their investors a return of nearly 5% over the past 12 months, which is incredibly high when you consider that the companies listed on the S&P 500 offered their investors an average return of -12% over the same time period.

We are on the brink of the fourth industrial revolution which will see the amalgamation of our physical, digital, and biological worlds through advances in robotics, artificial intelligence, and cloud computing. Technology plays an increasingly large role in our day to day lives, and it's undoubted that it will take over even more of the functions which we currently perform over the next decade. Technology companies are the vessels that will get us there. Their role in our ever-advancing world means that it's safe to assume that they'll keep growing in size and wealth.

The safest technology companies to invest in are those that are well established like Amazon, Alphabet, Netflix, Microsoft, Spotify, and Facebook. These companies have all been around for decades, and have been steadily growing in size and increasing in profitability since their inception.

Amazon's owner, Jeff Bezos, became the richest person in the world due to its success, and many analysts believe that it has yet to reach its full potential, which means there's still a lot of money to be made. Amazon's stocks reached a 52-week low in March of 2020, which means that they're currently relatively cheap to purchase, but Amazon is set to experience another upswing any day now. The outbreak of COVID-19 (and subsequent country-wide lockdowns) has caused an enormous surge in online purchases, which means that Amazon is sitting pretty. Researchers believe that people's shopping habits may never revert back to normal after the COVID-19 outbreak and that the tendency to shop online may change the retail landscape forever — Amazon is thus positioned to receive a further influx of customers over the next couple of years.

Alphabet has been Google's holding company since about 2015, and it's another technology company that's set to be a major role player in the stock exchanges of the future. A hefty portion of Google's profits are generated through advertising, so it's promising to know that nearly three-quarters of all internet searches are conducted on Google. As internet access becomes a global phenomenon, Google's customer base has steadily increased, and it's expected to continue to do so as third world countries improve their connectivity and the global population increases. Alphabet's income has also steadily been increasing by approximately 20% per annum over the past couple of years. People won't stop using search engines any time soon, which means that the future of Google (and thus Alphabet) is pretty much guaranteed to be bright. Alphabet stocks are the stocks for you if you're comfortable with paying a bit more for a share that you know will exponentially appreciate in value over the next 10 years.

Netflix is another technology company that you might want to consider investing in if you're trying to keep up with the technology sector. Netflix started out in 1997 as a DVD rental service that operated through the mail, but today it's an entertainment giant that creates its own original content with hundreds of millions of subscribers. It's likely that Netflix will continue innovating and reinventing itself (especially if you consider what it has achieved in the 23 years since its creation) which means that it's likely to keep up with the times by investing in new technologies. This innovative spirit is exactly what makes Netflix a good investment because it means that they're still striving to increase their business's reach and influence (which bodes well for future stock prices). Much like is the case with Alphabet stocks, Netflix stocks have benefited from the COVID-19 outbreak. The increase in people staying home (and the subsequent increase of people looking for entertainment at home) has boosted Netflix's viewership to unprecedented levels. It's unlikely that all of these newly acquired viewers will be lost after the outbreak ends, which means that this unfortunate period in human history has probably catered for a permanent increase in Netflix's value. The ever-growing population, and the expansion of the company itself to more international locations, ensures that Netflix's stock will continue to outperform most others over the coming decades.

Microsoft has been well-respected in the stock market since well before the dot-com bubble burst, but that doesn't mean that it's outdated or no longer relevant. Not only is Microsoft a permanent part of the technology sector's landscape, but its stocks are relatively cheap to acquire (at the moment one of Microsoft's shares is worth about half of one of Netflix's shares). Microsoft has become a pioneer in cloud data storage and processing, and is actively working on further improving this technology. This bodes well for Microsoft's future stock prices as the demand for cloud data storage is set to soar as businesses start doing away with the practice of storing information on hardware.

Of course, you don't have to invest in a 'tech giant' like Amazon or Microsoft in order to be successful in the stock market, many cheaper stocks are good investments too (remember that most of the companies on the S&P 500 started off by trading as penny stocks). Three of the best pink sheet technology stocks currently trading belong to Micro Focus International, Weidai Limited, and Cheetah Mobile.

Micro Focus International is a company that creates software that helps businesses with self-analysis. Its already-cheap stock prices have been driven down even further by the economic recession caused by COVID-19, which means that a share in this company will currently cost you less than $5. This is an absolute bargain if you consider that this company's price-to-earnings ratio is 1:3 (which means that you can expect to earn $3 for each dollar that you invest in this company).

A share in Weidai Limited will set you back less than $2, and this emerging technology company is set to maintain its upward trajectory for many years to come, which means that its current stock price represents an opportunity to pick up shares in one of the future's top technology companies for next to nothing. Weidai

Limited has created an online platform which connects those looking to borrow money with companies which offer suitable loans. Demand for this kind of service is set to increase during and after the COVID-19 outbreak as individuals and companies scramble to secure finance in order to continue their operations after the various international lockdowns. Not only is this company's rate of capital appreciation set to increase over the next couple of years, but it currently also offers a price-to-earnings ratio of 1:3.

Cheetah Mobile is a company which is based in China that develops mobile applications like games and photo editing software. Its stock price is currently just over $2, but it has peaked at over $4 over the past 12 months. The most appealing aspect of owning shares in this company is the 1:7 price-to-earnings ratio which it offers. Analysts estimate that Cheetah Mobile's earnings will increase by more than 100% per year over the next three years. Cheetah Mobile is a viable option for investors with shallow pockets who are looking to make a decent sum of money from dividends while watching the value of their investment increase over time.

Regardless of whether you choose to invest in clean energy or technology, one thing's certain — there's profit to be made if you're brave enough to invest despite the uncertain times we're currently living in. Now is the best time to buy shares cheaply before their prices recover after the COVID-19 market crash.

Chapter 2:

How Does the Stock

Market Work?

For many of us, the stock market is nothing but a collection of red and green percentages and their corresponding tickers (stock symbols) flashing on a computer screen, but how many of us really know how it works?

Ignorance certainly isn't bliss (not when you're dealing with the stock market anyway). Understanding how the stock market is analyzed and knowing all of the different investment types available to you will help you to plan and structure your possible future investments.

How the Stock Market is Analyzed

Smart investors thoroughly scrutinize stocks before buying them, and you should too. You should never research a stock in isolation though, it's important to compare any stock you're considering investing into similar stocks from the same sector.

The simplest way to research a stock is to review the company it belongs to's research report (which should be available along with the rest of the company's annual financial report). Companies usually publish research reports which contain metrics and graphs pertaining to the company's past, current, and expected performance.

Analyst reports are also a good starting point. These are regularly published by major investment banks and serve as a tool to help investors track stocks that have been performing well, as well as informing them of any market speculations in a particular sector

When analyzing a stock, investors need to further research the sector it belongs to's performance, the efficacy of its holding company's business model, its financial strength, the quality of its holding company's management, and its projected growth.

Analysts believe that you can predict a stock's future price or performance by studying its history. All analysis operates under the assumption and acceptance of two universal truths: the stock prices move up and down in set patterns (forming trends), and that history repeats itself (which means that the aforementioned patterns repeat themselves.

Analysts use market indicators in order to try to predict what the stock market will do next. Market indicators are formulas, ratios, and percentages that indicate the upward or downward movement of the stock market. They can even be used to predict whether stock market indexes are entering a bullish or bearish period. Some of the market indicators which investors make us of are price-to-earnings ratios, earnings per share, price-to-earnings growth (PEG) ratios, price-to-book ratios, and returns on equity.

Price-to-earnings ratios reflect how much investors can expect to spend and profit on each stock. If a company has a price-to-earnings ratio of 1:3, it means that you can expect to spend one dollar for every three dollars you earn on a specific stock. Companies with lower price-to-earnings ratios are generally seen as better investments.

A stock's 'earnings per share' indicates how many dollars an investor can expect to earn in dividends and payouts from it. When a stock's earnings per share increases, its stock price increases as well (which means that you can predict when a stock's price is about to rise by keeping an eye on its earnings per share).

PEG ratios are calculated by taking a company's price to earnings ratio and dividing it by the company's growth (which needs to have been extrapolated from a 12-month period). The best stocks to invest in have a PEG ratio of one or less.

Price-to-book ratios are calculated by taking a stock's real price and dividing it by its holding company's book price. A company's book price is calculated by taking its total liabilities and subtracting them from its total assets. If a company has a low price-to-book ratio, it's probably a good idea to scoop it up because it indicates that the stock is undervalued (which means that the market will realize its true value soon enough, which offers you an opportunity to 'buy low and sell high' — as traders say).

Returns on equity is another formula which investors use in order to determine whether a stock could potentially offer a steady stream of revenue. It is calculated by taking the net income of the stock and dividing it by the shareholders' average equity. A stock that shows a continual increase in its returns on equity is usually a good choice to invest in.

There are two different kinds of technical analysis which investors can employ in order to gauge a stock's future performance: top-down and bottom-up analysis. Top-down analysis involves first scrutinizing the stock's entire country of origin's economy, then the performance of the sector which it belongs to, and lastly the predicted growth of the individual stock itself. It is usually used by short-term investors. Bottom-up analysis involves first scrutinizing the predicted growth of the stock itself, before considering the sector or country which it belongs to. It is normally used by long-term investors.

Investors try to predict whether a stock's price will increase or decrease through analyzing candlestick charts. Candlestick charts reflect the market's joint sentiment towards a particular stock by plotting out its daily performances over a period of time, and indicate through the shape of the 'candlestick' (the icon used in such a chart) and its color how much that stock's price has fluctuated during the trading day. They also indicate the stock's high, low, opening, and closing price over a specific trading day.

Candlestick charts were invented in Japan in the 1700s by a rice trader named Munehisa Homma. Munehisa developed these charts in order to analyze the profitability of rice trading contracts based on the sentiments of those who invested in them. It took the Western world hundreds of years to catch up as the idea was only introduced to it in 1989 after Steve Nison penned an article on them in *Futures* magazine.

'Candlesticks' (icons that resemble rectangles with single lines sticking out of their short sides) represent a specific company's daily performances on a candlestick chart. If the rectangular part of the candlestick that you're observing is empty (or green), it means that the stock's price was higher at the stock exchange's close than it was at its open (the opposite is true if the rectangular part of the candlestick is filled or red). The line at the top of the candlestick (which is called a 'wick) represents the stock's highest trading price — the longer it is, the later in the trading day the stock reached its highest price. The bottom wick represents the stock's lowest trading price — the longer it is, the earlier in the trading day the stock reached its lowest price.

Analysts have observed a number of patterns that regularly appear in candlestick charts and have been able to make a few observations pertaining to what their appearance generally means for a stock's price.

The first pattern is called a 'bearish engulfing pattern' and analysts have realized that its appearance generally means that a stock's price is going to start experiencing a downswing. This pattern consists of a smaller empty (or green) candlestick followed by a much larger filled (or red) candlestick.

Another candlestick chart pattern is the 'bullish engulfing pattern' (which is basically the opposite of the bearish engulfing pattern described above). This pattern is good news for investors because it means that the stock's price is likely to increase. It is characterized by a smaller filled (or red) candlestick which is followed by a larger empty (or green) candlestick.

A 'bearish evening star' is a candlestick chart pattern that tells investors that a stock is about to exit an uptrend in its market price (in other words, a stock that has been doing well and increasing in value is about to start decreasing in value again). A bearish evening star is characterized by three candles in a specific order: a large empty (or green) candlestick, followed by a candlestick with a small body (the rectangular part of it is tiny), which is followed by a red candle of any shape or size.

The pattern called a 'bearish harami' indicates that a stock that's recently increased in price is about to backtrack and decrease in price again. Bearish haramis consist of one long empty (or green) candlestick followed by one short filled (or red) candlestick. In order for it to be a true bearish harami pattern, the filled (or red) candlestick needs to be short enough that its top and bottom wick fit within the boundaries of the empty (or green) candlestick.

A 'bullish harami' is essentially an inverted bearish harami. This pattern is present when a candlestick chart shows a smaller empty (or green) candlestick plotted to the left of a much larger filled (or red) candlestick. Just as is the case with bearish haramis, the smaller of the two candlesticks needs to be able to fit entirely (wicks and all) into the larger candlestick in order for the pattern to be a true bullish harami. A bullish harami indicates that the security it belongs to is a good investment because it is usually believed to mean that a stock that has been experiencing decreasing stock prices is about to experience an upswing and start increasing in value again.

A 'bullish rising three' pattern indicates that a stock is currently going through a bullish phase. This pattern consists of one long empty candlestick followed by three shorter filled candlesticks that are arranged in a downwards sloping pattern with another long empty (or green) candlestick to their right. The first of the three filled candlesticks shouldn't be higher than the uppermost point of the first long empty candlestick, and the third of the three filled candlesticks shouldn't be lower than the bottom-most point of the first long empty candlestick. The best time to invest in a stock that is going through a bullish rising three pattern is by buying into it on the day that it displays the third of its three filled candlesticks (which means you need to be able to spot a potential bullish rising three pattern before it's even complete).

The opposite of a bullish rising three pattern is a 'bearish falling three' pattern. This pattern is characterized by one long filled candlestick, followed by three short empty candlesticks arranged in an upwards sloping pattern with another long filled candlestick to their right. This pattern shows investors that a certain stock is going through a bearish phase. It's a good idea to invest in stocks that are going through a bearish phase if you're relatively sure that they'll start recovering again soon.

A 'hammer' pattern forms when a candlestick with a short body, long bottom wick, and no (or very short) top wick is found at the bottom of a number of candlesticks arranged in a downward slope. This pattern tells investors that an increase in demand for a certain stock has increased its stock price leading to it entering a bullish phase. Additionally, if the candlestick with a short body, long bottom wick, and no (or very short) top wick (known as the 'hammer') is empty it indicates that the stock is entering a more intense bullish phase than a filled candlestick would indicate.

An 'inverse hammer' pattern occurs when a candlestick with a short body, no (or very short) top wick, and long bottom wick is found at the bottom of a number of candlesticks arranged in a downward slope. The appearance of this pattern means that the supply of the stock will soon exceed demand, which will consequently lead to a dip in the stock's price. Smart investors who anticipate that this type of pattern is forming are quick to offload their affected short term stocks in order to avoid making a loss on their sale later on.

A 'piercing line' pattern consists of a long filled candlestick next to a long empty candlestick. This pattern indicates that a stock that has been experiencing a sustained downwards trend is about to experience a sudden spike in its market price. This sudden spike in its market price offers short-term investors the chance to sell the affected stocks before their market price starts declining again.

A 'three white soldiers' pattern is characterized by three long empty (or green) candlesticks arranged in an upward slope (each positioned slightly higher up on the chart than the former). This pattern shows investors that a stock is experiencing a surge in demand which may lead to a sustained bull market.

A 'hanging man' pattern occurs when a filled hammer with a very short top wick and a long bottom wick is present after a number of empty (or green) candlesticks. The appearance of this candlestick chart pattern generally means that the stock is about to transition from trading in a bullish market to trading in a bearish market, which means that its stock price is likely to start decreasing too.

A 'shooting star' pattern is present when a filled inverted hammer (a candlestick with a long top wick and a very short bottom wick) can be found at the top of an upward slope consisting of empty candlesticks. This pattern also indicates that a stock is going to start experiencing a decline in price.

How Stock Market Indices Work

Stock market indices were defined in the subsection titled 'Getting to Know the Lingo' in chapter one. They're basically 'companies' which measure the overall income (or loss) of a selection of stocks on a specific stock market.

The three most prolific stock market indices are the S&P 500, the Nasdaq Composite, and the Dow Jones Industrial Average.

The Nasdaq Composite comprises a number of companies chosen to represent the 2,500 other companies that are traded on the Nasdaq. Real estate investment trusts, common stocks, American depository receipts, limited partnership interests, and trading stock are all bought and sold on the Nasdaq, which means that the subsection which the index represents is incredibly diverse (although the Nasdaq Composite is probably best used to gauge the performance of technology companies as over 50% of the stock traded on the Nasdaq belongs to these companies).

The value of the Nasdaq is determined by taking the combined weight of its shares, multiplying it with their average closing price, and dividing the total by the index's divisor (this is a number which is chosen during the creation of a stock market index which is used to divide the numbers above into smaller, more manageable chunks). This value is recalculated and re-reported, with the last value before close being given at precisely 4:16 pm every day.

The companies which the Nasdaq Composite consists of are all American companies that are publicly traded on the Nasdaq. The Nasdaq Composite excludes equities like convertible debentures, preferred stocks, warrant, units, closed-end funds, and exchange-traded funds.

As mentioned above, half of the companies in the Nasdaq Composite are technology companies, while another fifth is made up of consumer services, and a tenth is made up of companies belonging to the health sector.

The Dow Jones Industrial Average (DJIA) consists of about 30 companies belonging to some of the most successful and profitable companies on the NYSE and Nasdaq. These 30 companies have been changed around, supplemented, or added to about 51 times over the DJIA's long history. Some of the stocks in the DJIA belong to the Walt Disney Company, Apple, American Express, Boeing, Coca-Cola, Walmart, The Home Depot, Pfizer, McDonalds, Microsoft, and Nike. The value of the DJIA is calculated by taking the total value of the shares in it and dividing them by an index divisor known as the 'Dow Divisor'.

Standard and poor aren't just terms used to refer to the lifestyles of those that don't seize the opportunity to invest in the stock market, it's a stock market index too. The Standard and Poor 500 (S&P 500) consists of the 500 most prolific American stocks. The value of the S&P 500 is calculated by adding together the market capitalizations of all of the stocks in it and dividing the resulting total by a divisor.

In summation, stock market indices are a tool that you, as an investor, can use to gauge the health and trajectory of the stock market.

How Mutual Funds Work

Mutual funds were also defined in chapter one. In short, they're companies that you can buy into that make their money by buying and selling shares through the stock market. Mutual funds only trade after the stock market has closed for the day, which means that you won't be able to buy them at the spur of the moment on the NYSE or Nasdaq. These mutual funds are run by managers who are motivated to increase the fund's returns because their own income depends on how profitable the fund is.

There are four distinct kinds of mutual funds. The first kind are called money market funds. Money market funds invest in cash equivalent shares (shares that are meant to be short term investments) like United States' treasuries, commercial paper, certificates of deposit, banker's acceptances, and repurchase agreements. They also make up about a sixth of all mutual funds.

There are four further kinds of money market funds: tax-exempt money market funds, government money market funds, treasury money market funds, and prime money market funds.

Tax-exempt money market funds usually invest in debt securities like municipal bonds. They earned their name because they're not subject to U.S. income tax (with some even being totally or partially exempt from municipal taxes too).

Government money market funds buy and sell government securities. Government securities are investments that governments sell in order to help them fund their own operation with the promise of full repayment plus interest when the security matures. Government securities are basically a way for the government to borrow money from investors.

Treasury money market funds are similar to government money market funds. They trade in debt securities issued by the U.S. Treasury (like bonds, notes, and bills).

Prime money market funds are money market funds which are not tax-exempt, nor are their main assets government or treasury securities. They trade in commercial paper (securities sold by companies in order to finance their operations, payroll, or short term liabilities) and variable-rate debt. One of the best prime money market funds to invest in is the Vanguard Prime Money Market Fund (VMMXX). A single share in VMMXX trades for as little as $1, though you need to initially invest at least $3,000 in order to 'buy in'.

Balanced funds are the second kind of mutual fund. They are made out of three components: a money market component, a bonds component, and a stock component. Balanced funds try to strike a balance between investing in equity and investing in debt (this constant tightrope-act is how they acquired their name). This kind of mutual fund is relatively low risk and has low expense ratios. The Vanguard Balanced Index Fund (VBINX) is an example of a balanced fund (and it boasts a returns rate of nearly 10%).

The third kind of mutual fund is known as a bond fund. Bond funds do exactly what their name says they do: they buy and sell bonds. A bond is a type of loan that you make to a business. Businesses sell bonds as a method of financing in order to increase their cash flow. In exchange for buying one of these bonds, investors can expect regular payments (with interest) on the money they've loaned to said business. Bond funds are even lower risk than balanced funds because a bond never decreases in value (unless the company that issues it goes bankrupt).

The final kind of mutual fund is called a stock fund. Stock funds' portfolios mostly consist of individual shares in companies that are publicly traded on one of the major stock exchanges. Many investors shy away from investing in stock funds, opting to rather invest in specific individual shares, because investing through a stock fund can deprive you of the ownership you would have otherwise had (when you buy individual stocks, you own a portion of the company, but when you invest in a stock fund, you only own a piece of that specific stock fund — and not the stocks it has invested in).

Mutual fund managers make their money by asking investors to pay a 'load' (a sales fee) when first buying into the fund, as well as charging a level-load fee annually (this sum is subtracted from the fund's assets). Some mutual funds also charge a 12b-1 fee on top of the bid price of every share they sell, and most charge additional administrative fees too.

The best mutual funds you can currently invest in are the DWS Large Cap Focus Growth Fund (which has a five-year average return of nearly 16%), the PGIM Jennison Focused Growth Fund (which has a five-year average return of nearly 17%), and the T. Rowe Price New America Growth Fund (which has a five-year average return of just over 16%).

How Stock Market Index Funds Work

Remember the stock market indices we discussed earlier (like the S&P 500 or the DJIA)? Well, index funds work by trying to mimic them. Index fund managers scoop up stocks represented on the index fund's index of choice, thus ensuring that the index fund performs in exactly the same way as the index itself. These kinds of funds are described as being 'passive' because they are not constantly buying and selling stocks (most of the main companies on the major stock exchanges are relatively constant and stable, which means that index funds don't need to switch up their portfolios too often).

The billionaire, Warren Buffett, recommends that investors ensure that index funds make up a large portion of their 401(k) accounts or individual retirement accounts, stating that he believes that they are the ideal 'sunset investment'. It is usually cheaper to invest in an index fund than it is to invest in a mutual fund because index funds save money (and thus require less of it from investors) by not needing the services of research analysts. Index funds don't need research analysts because their managers simply follow the trends set by their chosen stock market index, whereas other funds need to put quite a bit of consideration into which stocks they choose to buy.

Some of the top best index funds to currently invest in are the Schwab S&P 500 Index Fund (SWPPX), Fidelity

ZERO Large Cap Index (FNILX), Fidelity NASDAQ Composite Index (FNCMX), and the Schwab Total Stock Market Index (SWTSX).

The Schwab S&P 500 Index Fund is one of the smaller popular index funds, but don't let that put you off because it has been outperforming its competitors for nearly 24 years. Not only has it proven incredibly profitable under the Charles Schwab's guidance (an investor who has set up one of the most successful American investment firms and is worth billions himself), but its expense ratio is incredibly low too at 0.02% (which means it'll cost you $0.20 a year to invest $1,000 dollars in this fund).

The Fidelity ZERO Large Cap Index is another fantastic choice for investors who are looking for a dependable investment. This fund mimics the Fidelity U.S. Large Cap Index, which is very similar to the S&P 500 index. The Fidelity ZERO Large Cap Index is even cheaper to invest in than the Schwab S&P 500 Index Fund with an expense ratio of zero (which accounts for the ZERO in its name).

The Fidelity NASDAQ Composite Index consists of a number of 'large cap' companies (companies with large market capitalizations), most of which belong to the health or technology sector. This index fund's expense ratio is 0.3% which means that if you invest $1,000 dollars in it every year, it'll cost you an additional $3.

The Schwab Total Stock Market Index's portfolio tries to mimic the entire stock market instead of focusing on a specific index. It's also one of the cheaper index funds to join with a buy-in of just $1,000. It also has a relatively low expense ratio of 0.02%, which makes it perfect for first time investors.

Index funds offer investors the chance to automatically diversify their portfolios with one simple buy-in, while keeping their fees low (meaning you'll need less cash on hand in order to manage your investment after it's made). Regardless of your motivations, index funds are a smart investment for nearly every investor.

How Exchange-Traded Funds Work

Exchange-traded funds (ETFs) are so called because they trade in the stock exchange. They are a lot like mutual funds in the sense that they pool investors' money in order to buy and sell securities like stocks, commodities, and bonds. Unlike mutual funds, portions of them are traded in the stock market like shares. While mutual funds only trade after the stock market has closed, ETF shares are for sale throughout the entire trading day.

There are five different kinds of ETFs, namely bond ETFs, commodity ETFs, industry ETFs, currency ETFs, and inverse ETFs.

Bond ETFs specifically invest in (you guessed it) bonds. The fact that they trade in the stock market like ordinary stocks differentiates them from bond mutual funds (this is essentially the most significant difference between ETFs and mutual funds). Bond funds are more liquid than mutual funds (or even individual stocks) which makes them one of the few relatively recession-proof investments you can make in the stock market. They are also the ideal investment for investors who would like regular payouts from their investments because they pay out interest to investors monthly, and dividends annually, which means that you're guaranteed to have a near-constant stream of income from them.

Some of the best bond ETFs to invest in are the iShares iBoxx Investment Grade Corporate Bond ETF (LQD), the SPDR (pronounced 'spider') Portfolio Short Term Corporate Bond ETF (SPSB), the Pimco 0-5 Year High Yield Corporate Bond ETF (HYS), and the Invesco International Corporate Bond ETF (PICB).

The iShares iBoxx Investment Grade Corporate Bond ETF is one of the larger bond ETFs. It consists of thousands of bonds, with nearly a quarter belonging to the banking sector, and possesses more than $35 billion in assets. Some of the major companies which feature in this fund's portfolio are the Comcast Corporation and J.P. Morgan. It also boasts a price-to-earnings ratio of 1:17 which means that you can expect to earn $17 for every one dollar you spend on this fund.

The SPDR Portfolio Short Term Corporate Bond ETF is a low-risk investment because it only buys up bonds that are within three years of their expiration date. Just because it's low risk doesn't mean that it doesn't strive to make its investors as much money as possible, in fact, this fund mainly trades in bonds issued by Goldman Sachs and the Oracle Corporation. It is also one of the cheapest bond ETFs to buy into, with a stock price which is currently just over $30, which makes it the perfect investment for first-time investors.

The Pimco 0-5 Year High Yield Corporate Bond ETF invests in corporate bonds with high returns that are within five years of maturation, thus it's considered a high return, low-risk investment. Being both high return and low-risk means that it's in high demand too, which means that this fund doesn't feel the need to squirm away from asking fees that are slightly higher than the norm (its expense ratio is 0.56%). Luckily shares in this ETF are reasonable prices (they're currently selling for $85).

The Invesco International Corporate Bond ETF is a great fund to invest in if you don't want to hedge all of your bets on the American economy because its portfolio also consists of international bonds (unfortunately, this also means that its returns are slightly lower because international bonds tend to have lower interest rates attached to them). Luckily these slightly lower returns are reflected in this fund's stock price (which is currently trading for just under $25).

Commodity ETFs buy and sell commodity stocks. Commodity stocks belong to companies that produce or work with commodities, like the mining and agricultural sectors. Commodity ETFs are one of the best investments to own during a recession because stock prices and commodity prices are inversely related — when stock prices drop, commodity prices rise, and vice versa.

The best commodity ETFs for beginner investors to invest in are the First Trust Global Tactical Commodity Strat ETF (FTGC), the iPath Pure Beta Broad Commodity ETN (BCM), and the Invesco DB Commodity Tracking Fund (DBC).

The First Trust Global Tactical Commodity Strat ETF doesn't trade in everyday commodities, instead, its portfolio is largely made up of live cattle, cocoa beans, and soybean oil. It is actively managed which means that this fund's manager is constantly buying and selling securities, instead of investing in long term securities and sitting on them. Unfortunately, being actively managed also means that its fees are higher than normal. It has an expense ratio of about 0.95% which means that investing in this fund will cost you an additional $9.50 for an annual investment of $1,000. Fortunately, you can save some money on this fund's stock price which is currently a humble $14.

The iPath Pure Beta Broad Commodity ETN trades in commodities that are featured on the Barclays Commodities Index. The majority of this fund's portfolio is made up of securities in companies that mine or deal in precious metals. This fund is currently trading at $22 per share, which is a fair price for such a successful stock. Its success is enhanced by the fact that its core investment, precious metals, is constantly increasing in value. Its expense ratio is only 0.75%

which is significantly lower than the former commodity fund which was discussed.

The Invesco DB Commodity Tracking Fund is the cheapest of the three commodity funds. Its portfolio mainly consists of shares in energy companies, though it actively strives to diversify its stocks in gold and silver. Although its stock price is the lowest (it is currently at just below $12), its expense ratio is average at best (at 0.89%).

Industry ETFs are also known as sector ETFs. They trade in shares that belong to one specific sector of the economy. Some of the sectors which industry ETFs might operate in are energy, industrials, materials, real estate, utilities, information technology, telecommunication services, healthcare, financials, and consumer staples. Shares in industry ETFs are incredibly liquid (they're easy to buy and easy to sell) which means that they seldomly underperform when compared to related stock exchange indices.

There are numerous industry ETFs to invest in, though the two most popular ones have proven to be the Vanguard Consumer Staples ETF (VDC) and the Global X MSCI China Large-Cap 50 ETF (CHIL).

The Vanguard Consumer Staples ETF's shares currently trade for nearly $140, has an expense ratio of only 0.1% and its price to earnings ratio is about 1:9 (which means you should plan to spend an additional $9 for every one dollar you that invest), making it one of the more expensive ETFs to invest in. Consumer staples hardly, if ever, experience downswings — which means that this fund is a stable, dependable investment. This fund owns shares from 93 different stocks (99% of which are American) which focus on sectors like packaged food, soft drinks, meats, and household products. These shares feature major name brands which include Walmart, Coca-Cola, Pepsi. Co, and Procter and Gamble.

If you don't have the necessary funds to invest in the Vanguard Consumer Staples ETF, you should consider investing in the Global X MSCI China Large-Cap 50 ETF. This fund's stocks are currently selling for about $120 cheaper than the former ETF's stocks are. The Global X MSCI China Large-Cap 50 ETF trades in shares issued by China's most successful businesses. Shockingly it has been able to offer its investors returns of up to 25% over the past year, making it one of the most profitable industry ETFs. While the Vanguard Consumer Staples ETF is the more constant of the two, the Global X MSCI China Large-Cap 50 ETF is the right option for investors who want to make a lot of money quickly.

Currency ETFs are the perfect option for investors who would like to invest in forex (short for 'foreign exchange') but who don't want to take the risk of investing in individual foreign currencies themselves. These funds buy and sell currencies as their exchange rates fluctuate in order to make an income. Some currency ETFs only trade in one or two currencies, while others trade in as many as six (it's up to investors to research currency ETFs' portfolios and decide which one suits their needs best).

Some of the best multi-currency ETFs are the Barclay's iPath Optimized Currency Carry ETN (ICI), the WisdomTree Dreyfus Commodity Currency Fund (CCX), and the iShares Emerging Markets Local Currency Bond Fund (LEMB). If you're looking for a currency ETF that specifically trades in British Pounds you should consider the CurrencyShares British Pound Sterling Trust (FXB), if you're looking to invest in in the Japanese Yen you should look into the ProShares UltraShort Yen ETF (YFS), or perhaps you'd like to invest in the Euro, in which case you should consider investing in the ProShares Ultra Euro ETF (ULE) or the CurrencyShares Euro Trust ETF (FXE).

The final kind of ETF is called an inverse ETF (they're also known as 'short' or 'bear' ETFs). Inverse ETFs are designed to make money when the stock market starts underperforming and trading below average. They manage to do this by borrowing stocks from traders and then selling them just before the market dips so that they can repurchase them for even cheaper than they would have paid for them through a trader. One of the downsides of inverse ETFs is that they tend to charge higher fees. Not only will you pay more to have your investment managed in an inverse ETF, it's also much higher risk (if you don't buy in just before the market experiences a downswing you stand to lose an awful lot of money) — for this reason, they're not the ideal investment for those who are still familiarizing themselves with the stock market and stock trading.

Inverse ETF funds usually track a certain stock market index (a bit like index funds), but instead of mimicking their value, they 'inverse' it. In other words, if the index the inverse ETF is tracking falls by 10%, the inverse ETF itself grows by 10%). There are index funds that offer even higher returns called double and triple inverse funds, and they do exactly what their names say they do. If the index a double inverse fund is tracking falls by 10%, the double inverse fund grows by 20%. If the index a triple inverse fund is tracking falls by 10%, the triple inverse fund grows by 30%.

If you suspect that there's an emerging bear market, you should consider investing in ProShares Short QQQ (PSQ), Direxion Daily S&P 500 High Beta Bear 3X Shares (HIBS), and Direxion Daily Dow Jones Internet Bear 3X Shares (WEBS). Both Direxion Daily S&P 500 High Beta Bear 3X Shares (which tracks the S&P 500 index) and Direxion Daily Dow Jones Internet Bear 3X Shares (which tracks the Dow Jones) are triple inverse funds which means that they potentially offer returns that are three times higher than those offered by normal inverse funds.

How Hedge Funds Work

Hedge funds were defined in chapter one. They're similar to mutual funds in the sense that they pool investors' money in order to make investments which will generate income for its investors, and they're similar to inverse ETFs in the sense that they strive to beat the market even when it's down. The difference is that your average Joe can buy into a mutual fund or an inverse ETF, while you need to be an incredibly successful, accredited investor (who meets specific criteria) in order to buy into a hedge fund. Most hedge funds require that their investors have a yearly income of no less than $200,000 or a net worth of at least $1 million each. Hedge funds are also highly unregulated because 99% of them don't need to register with or comply with the U.S. Securities Exchange Commission (SEC).

Hedge funds are designed for wealthy investors with years of experience in trading stocks, so they're understandably also more expensive than most other kinds of stock market investments. Most hedge funds follow a 2:20 fee structure which means that their managers take 20% of all of the profit that you make, as well as charging a further management fee which is equal to 2% of the value of all of the assets held within the fund.

There are four distinct types of hedge funds: distressed hedge funds, equity hedge funds, relative value arbitrage hedge funds, and macro hedge funds.

Distressed hedge funds invest in what is known as 'distressed debt.' This is debt that belongs to companies that are on the brink of financial ruin. Hedge funds buy distressed debt at enormous discounts from companies which they believe will be able to make a turnaround and recover from their predicament. The distressed hedge funds that are currently ranked first, second, and third in terms of their profitability are Aurelius Capital, Oaktree Capital, and Elliott Associates.

Equity hedge funds, which are also known as long or short hedge funds, split their portfolio by holding a few long-position stocks and a few short-position stocks (long- and short-position are defined in chapter one under 'Getting to Know the Lingo' — refresh your memory if you don't remember what these terms mean). The three top performing equity hedge funds of 2019 were the Blackrock Long Short Equity Fund, the AQR Long-Short Equity N, and the Locorr Long Short Equity Fund.

Relative value arbitrage hedge funds invest in two kinds of stocks: those that they believe are overvalued and those that they believe are undervalued. They sell the stocks that they believe are overvalued (and may repurchase them at a later date when their prices have decreased) and buy up stocks which they believe to be undervalued in order to sell them once their prices have increased. These two types of stocks are usually related (either by belonging to the same sector or by featuring on the same stock market index), which is why 'relative value arbitrage' is often called 'pairs trading'. Some of the best relative value arbitrage hedge funds are Carmot Capital and the Sabre Style Arbitrage Fund.

Macro hedge funds analyze the global economy (also known as the 'macroeconomy') and then invest in stocks that will be profitable if their predictions about the global market's performance are correct. Three of the best macro hedge funds to invest in currently are Soros Fund Management, Caxton Associates, and Bridgewater Associates.

Chapter 3:

Understanding What A

Stock Actually Is

You'll remember from chapter one that stocks or shares are little pieces of companies that you can either buy over-the-counter or through a stock exchange. Stocks or shares can either be purchased individually or in bundles through a mutual fund, an index fund, an exchange-traded fund or a hedge fund. They also offer two potential streams of income to investors: capital appreciation (the increase of their value over time) and dividends.

Stocks or shares are the building blocks of the stock market, and thus it's important that you understand where they come from and why they're issued. It is equally important that you're able to differentiate between the different kinds of stocks.

Why Companies Sell Stocks

You might be wondering why companies choose to sell stocks in order to raise capital when doing so essentially dilutes the original owners' ownership of the company, but it's about a lot more than just giving the business a cash injection. If a company's stocks perform well, that company may qualify for bigger, better loans at lower interest rates.

Initial public offerings aren't the only way for publicly-traded companies to make money off of issuing stocks. Companies whose stocks are performing well often issue even more shares (called a secondary offering) in order to capitalize on the demand for their stocks. This means that companies don't view issuing stocks as a once-off capital generator, but as something which they can use to periodically increase their cash flow.

There is also a sense of prestige attached to the issuing of shares. 'Going public' is something that many business owners actively pursue (believing that they will have 'made it' if their company starts trading on the NYSE or Nasdaq).

The Difference Between Privately Traded Stocks and Publicly-Traded Stocks

All companies which sell their stocks on stock exchanges are publicly traded, but a company doesn't need to trade publicly in order to issue stocks. Private companies may also decide to sell shares to private investors without having to make an IPO (like publicly-traded companies have to).

Unfortunately, privately traded stocks can't be purchased by just anyone. Just as is the case with hedge funds, investors who invest in privately traded stocks need to be accredited. The requirements for accreditation include a minimum-income aspect (accredited investors either need to have a net worth of $1 million or need to earn $200,000 annually).

There are three different methods which can be used to sell stocks privately. The first is known as a private placement. Private placement involves selling stock to investors and investment firms which were selected and approved before the sale itself took place. Regulation D of the Securities Act of 1933 outlines all of the requirements of a legal private placement sale and states that such sales don't need to be registered with the SEC. Prospectuses and financial information also don't need to be provided by the holding company during this type of sale.

The second method is to structure your company as a limited partnership and charging all of the partners to the company a buy-in fee. The third method is similar to the first but involves structuring your business as a small corporation and selling shares to the members of the company.

Privately traded shares tend to be higher risk than publicly traded shares because there is no legislation which forces their holding companies to make their financial statements and position available to the public.

How Companies Sell Stocks

There are only two options which growing companies have when it comes to raising capital: go into debt or issue stocks. Many companies choose to issue stocks rather than taking out a loan (or loans). Issuing stocks is particularly attractive to new businesses which do not yet have a credit rating high enough to qualify for the class of loan which they'd need in order to meet their financing needs. Many companies are also wary of acquiring debt in general because it raises the value of their liabilities (which is something investors will look at when trying to decide whether or not to invest in the company).

Once a company has decided that the best way for it to raise capital is through issuing stocks, it needs to decide how many stocks to issue. It'll do this by deciding on the amount of money which it hopes to make from issuing stock and comparing this to the predicted value of its shares. If a company knows it needs to raise $100,000 and it knows that its stocks will sell for $10 per share, it can extrapolate that it would need to sell 10,000 shares. Of course, it's not that easy and this simple sum isn't the only guiding force behind the number of shares which companies can issue as the final deciding factor is the number of shares agreed to in the company's Articles of Incorporation (a document which is drawn up when the company is formed).

Once a company has decided how many shares it would like to issue, and at what price, it needs to draw up and submit a stock subscription agreement. Stock subscription agreements are basically contracts in which companies agree to sell stocks to investors at a certain price. Anyone who signs this stock subscription agreement, and thus buys shares in the company, also needs to be issued with a stock certificate.

How Companies Qualify to Sell Stocks on The Nasdaq and NYSE

Once a company has decided to issue shares, it needs to decide whether it's going to sell them 'over-the-counter' (as was defined in chapter one) or on one of the major stock exchanges.

There are a number of over-the-counter exchanges to choose from, each with its own unique listing requirements. One of the most popular over-the-counter exchanges is called the Best Market (OTCQX). In order to be listed on the OTCQX a company needs to have at least 50 current shareholders with a minimum of 100 shares each, it needs to have a market capitalization of $10 million at the time of its IPO (and it needs to maintain a market capitalization of at least $5 million to remain on the OTCQX), and its net tangible assets need to be more than $5 million if it has been operating for less than three years or more than $2 million if it has been operating for more than three years. Stocks listed on the OTCQX also need to have a stock price of at least $0.25 at the time of their IPO, and they need to maintain a price of $0.10 in order to remain listed.

The Venture Market (OTCQB) is another popular over-the-counter stock exchange. Companies that want to be listed on the OTCQB need to have a minimum of 50 shareholders who own at least 100 shares each (which is identical to the shareholder-size requirement set by the OTCQX). The stock price requirement is much lower on the OTCQB than it is on the OTCQX though, with companies only needing to sell their shares for a minimum of $0.10 at the time of their IPO. Companies listed on this exchange also need to have their finances audited by an auditor that is accredited by the Public Company Accounting Oversight Board.

The least regulated of the three most popular stock exchanges belonging to the OTC Market Group is the 'Pink Sheets' (which has been shortened to 'Pink'). There are no minimum requirements that a company needs to meet in order to sell their shares through this stock exchange, which means that it doesn't exclude delinquent companies, bankrupt companies, or companies that refuse to submit their annual financial reports to the public. All a company needs to do in order to be listed on this stock exchange is to complete and submit a Form 15C211.

Of course, most companies aim to list their stocks on one of America's two most influential stock exchanges: the NYSE or Nasdaq. It goes without saying that both of these stock exchanges have much more stringent entrance requirements than the over-the-counter stock exchanges that were discussed above.

A company needs to have a minimum of 400 current shareholders that own at least 100 shares each in order to qualify to be listed on the NYSE. It also needs to have issued a minimum of 1.1 million shares in total that have a combined value of at least $40 million. The company's share price can also not be less than $4 per share. Companies that want to be listed on the NYSE also need to either have a global market capitalization of $200 million or they need to have proved their profitability by making a profit of $10 million (before tax) every year for the past three years.

It's slightly easier to get listed on the Nasdaq. Companies that would like to be listed on the Nasdaq need to have a minimum bid price of $3 and their stocks need to be owned by a minimum of 300 different shareholders. The Nasdaq also requires that participating companies have a minimum of $4 million in total assets.

The Different Kinds of Stocks

There are two different kinds of stocks: common stocks and preferred stocks.

Common stocks are a fantastic long term investment. They are stocks which give their holder the right to vote on corporate policies, as well as granting him or her a say as to who gets elected to be a member of the board of directors. If you own shares and you're not sure which kind they are, they're likely to be common stocks.

There are, however, a few downsides to owning this kind of stock. Common stocks usually do not have fixed dividends. If they do pay out money to their holders it's usually in the form of sporadic, irregular payments. Common stockholders are also seen as being a rung lower on the obligations' ladder than owners of preferred stock are, which means that if the stock's holding company goes bankrupt, common stockholders are the last parties to get paid (if there's even enough money left to pay them after the company has been liquidated in order to pay its debts). Common stocks' values also tend to fluctuate more (which is why they're not ideal short term investments) which, in turn, causes their stock prices to be relatively unstable.

Preferred stocks do not come with voting rights as common stocks do, but they do offer fixed dividends which means that preferred stockholders are guaranteed to receive payouts either monthly or annually. In fact, when a company is recovering from financial problems it might stop making any sporadic payments which it previously would have made to common stockholders in order to pay its preferred stockholders. When companies are in so much financial trouble that they can't afford to pay any dividends, they may become indebted to preferred stockholders and have to pay them for any dividends which are in arrears once they recover. Another upside to preferred stocks is the fact that their stock prices are more stable than those of common stocks are. These kinds of stocks offer investors more income than common stocks do, and are thus a safer short term investment.

When a company declares bankruptcy, its assets are liquidated in order to pay back all of its debtors. Stockholders who own preferred stocks receive refunds on their investments along with other debtors, while common stockholders only receive refunds if there is any money left after the other debtors and preferred stockholders have been paid.

Companies may sub-divide their shares further by classifying them as either class A or class B shares. Class A shareholders usually have more voting rights than

Class B shareholders do. Common shares are normally called class A shares, while preferred stocks are normally classified as class B shares.

Why Stock Prices Fluctuate

For the largest part stock prices are determined by the supply and demand of a certain stock. If there are many buyers who would like to invest in a certain stock, but not many of those shares available, demand will push the stock's price up. On the other hand, if there are numerous shares belonging to a single company available for sale, but few potential buyers, oversupply will cause the stock's price to decline.

Surprisingly, financial institutions' interest rates may also affect the prices of stocks. When their interest rates are high, investors are less likely to seek out financing from them and are thus less likely to buy stocks. This decrease in demand causes stocks' prices to plummet. When their interest rates are low, investors are more willing to take out loans and in turn, they buy more stocks, which increases the stocks' demand. This increase in demand causes stock prices to rise.

What's happening on the news and in national or international politics can also influence a stock's price. Bad news (like a declaration of war, a natural disaster, the outbreak of a virus or disease, a terrorist attack, or a political scandal) seems to cause investors to sell their stocks and securities, which drives their prices down. Good news (like national economic growth, a favorable election outcome, or the end of a war) has the opposite effect, seemingly encouraging investors to buy bigger volumes of stocks than they normally would, consequently driving their prices up.

Smart investors learn how to use bad news to their advantage (because the period directly after it has been announced is bound to be characterized by lower stock prices, which means that it's the ideal time to buy). You need to be able to apply a good dose of logic in order to make money off of bad news, but it's entirely possible. For example, if a declaration of war is made it's the ideal time to invest in weapons manufacturing companies, as well as companies which are involved in producing the raw materials needed to manufacture weapons. On the other hand, if a contagious virus or disease breaks out you might want to invest in stocks belonging to healthcare companies as their stock prices are bound to skyrocket due to their holding companies' increased performance during this time period.

Professional investors try to anticipate the day's news before it breaks in order to stay ahead of the market. If an investor knows that the stock market is going to start declining before it actually starts declining it affords him or her the opportunity to offload some of his or her stocks at their original price (thus avoiding losing money on them when the declining stock market inevitably drives their prices down). Investors try to do this by keeping up with the latest government economic reports, company and industry news, and gossip.

Chapter 4:

Getting Started

Before you approach brokerage firms and open an account or make changes to your 401(k) account, you need to be able to decide which stocks you'd like to invest in and you need to know how much capital you can invest in them.

It's always tempting to simply invest in the companies that we've come to know and love (Microsoft, Apple, Amazon, or Facebook). While these companies are usually safe investments, there's more profit to be made in investing in upcoming stocks belonging to companies which have yet to reach their peak. In order to be able to spot upcoming stocks, you need to know how to research them, which necessitates the ability to read stock charts and stock quotes.

How to Research a Stock's Potential

Someone once told me that the easiest way to double one's money in the stock market was by folding it in half and putting it back in one's pocket — and this may very well be true if you're not willing to thoroughly research the stocks that you're investing in. Some stock market gurus even advise that investors focus on investing in companies which offer a service or produce a product that relates to something that they are interested in in order to make having to do research on the company more bearable. In other words, if you're a car fanatic you might want to look into investing in Honda, General Motors, or Fiat.

If you want to know whether a certain stock is going to increase or decrease in value (and by how much), you need to go all the way back to its source: its holding company.

As was discussed earlier, publicly-traded companies are required to submit reports pertaining to their financial position to the SEC every year. Luckily for investors, it's not hard to get your hands on anything from periodic reports to registration statements through the SEC's Electronic Data Gathering, Analysis, and Retrieval system (fondly dubbed 'EDGAR') which stores (and allows you to search for) publicly-traded companies' financial details and reports. You can access EDGAR online at www.sec.gov/edgar — upon accessing this link you'll see that the SEC also offers a quick free tutorial on how to use EDGAR to find the information that you're looking for.

The best document you can possibly find on EDGAR is a company's 10-k filing which contains information that has been independently verified by a third-party auditor pertaining to the company's financial performance over the past five years. This document also contains information pertaining to how the company generates its revenue, any threats which the company currently faces, any threats which it may face in the future, and any problems with its management.

The most significant thing EDGAR will be able to show you is a publicly-traded company's revenue. A company's revenue (measured over a specific period of time) tells investors whether that company has been making money. Companies that are continuously growing (and whose revenue increases after every measured period) are likely to have stocks that are also appreciating in value over time.

The financial reports which companies have to submit to the SEC also contain their earnings-per-share. This measurement is the best one to use when trying to surmise how much you can expect to profit off of any given share because it tells you (in a dollar value) how much income you can expect to receive from every stock that you own in a specific company.

You can also predict whether a company's share price is about to move up or down by keeping an eye on what its executives and managers are doing with their shares. They're likely to know of any hardships which a company may encounter long before the public is made aware of them, which means that when they start selling their stocks, it's time to start selling yours too before the news of whatever catastrophe occurred breaks

How to Read a Stock Chart

If you enter a company's stock symbol (ticker) into Google Finance or Yahoo Finance, it will bring up that company's stock chart. Stock charts are important research tools because they allow investors to see the 'bigger picture'. Simply checking stock prices will certainly keep you up to date with a stock's day-to-day price fluctuations, but it won't allow you to see whether the stock's price has been slowly declining over time, or whether it's entering a bull market.

A stock chart's plot-line shows investors what the stock sold for at different times. The chart's Y-axis represents the price which the stock sold for, while the chart's X-axis represents the day on which the stock sold for that price.

Some stock charts also have a feature (in the form of a bar chart just above the chart's x-axis) which enables you to extrapolate the number of shares sold in a specific company on a specific day. The volume of stocks sold on a specific day tells investors a lot about the market's sentiment towards that particular stock. If a high volume of stocks in a specific company are sold on a specific day, but their trading prices remain low, it might mean that the stock is about to enter a bearish phase.

You should also be able to see whether a company has split its stocks or paid out dividends at the bottom of the chart just above the stock volume's bar chart. This is valuable information to investors because stock splits cause the stock's price to decrease, while the regular payment of dividends usually causes it to increase.

Stock charts also display a stock's earnings per share and its holding company's market capitalization. More intricate stock charts may even indicate a company's performance estimates for the upcoming year.

How to Read a Stock Quote

A stock quote is a snippet of information which states the stock's current trading price, along with its last trade, trade time, change, previous close, open, bid and ask prices, one-year target, day's range, 52-week range, volume, average volume, market capitalization, price-to-earnings ratio, earnings per share, dividends, and its yield. It is usually laid out in two columns directly under the company's name and stock symbol.

The stock's last trade is usually the first bit of information listed in the left column of the stock quote. A stock's last trade indicates the amount of money a single share sold for most recently, which means that this value changes every time that a share is purchased. Consequently, this value is ever-changing and hard to keep track of.

The stock's trade time is indicated just below its last trade. It indicates when the sale that the last trade value is based upon took place.

The next value in the left column is 'change'. This value shows potential investors the difference between the stock's most recent trading price (last trade) and the price which it traded for directly before that sale.

Just below the stock's change, you'll find its previous close. This value is the price which the stock was trading at when the stock exchange closed on the previous day.

The next value in the left column is 'open'. This is the price which the stock was trading for when the stock exchange opened on the day that the quote was issued.

The stock's 'bid and ask' can usually be found just below its open, but it seldomly indicates any value other than N/A (not applicable). This is because the bid ask value is supposed to be comprised of the highest price which an investor is willing to pay for a stock and the lowest price that the seller of the stock is willing to sell it for, which makes it difficult to determine this value as very few brokers are willing to publicly announce the most amount of money that they're willing to pay for a share.

The final value in a stock quote's left-hand column is the stock's one-year target. This value is determined by an analyst hired by whomever drew up the stock quote and represents what that analyst believes the stock's price will be one year after the issuing of the quote. This value is speculative at best, and you should try not to base your decision to buy a stock solely on it.

The first value in a stock quote's right-hand column is the stock's day range. This value does exactly what its name says it does — it reflects the amount which a stock's price has fluctuated by on the day that the quote is issued. Stocks with smaller day ranges tend to be less volatile (and thus lower risk) than stocks with higher day ranges.

The second value in the right-hand column is the stock's 52-week range. This value indicates how much a stock's price has fluctuated over a one year period. Just as is the case with day ranges, the smaller a stock's 52-week range is, the more stable it is.

The next item is volume, which we know refers to the number of stocks traded on a particular day.

Just below volume is average volume. This value is usually measured over a three month time span and can be used to work out whether the volume (which is only measured over one trading day) is higher or lower than it usually is.

The next four values listed in the right-hand corner are the stock's market capitalization, price-to-earnings ratio, earnings per share, and dividends.

The final item at the bottom of the right-hand column is yield. A stock's yield takes the stock's dividends and displays them as a percentage of the stock's market price. You should be careful not to invest in stocks simply because they have a high yield because a high yield can also be a result of a rapidly declining stock price. A rapidly declining stock price might be a symptom of financial difficulties, and a company that is experiencing financial difficulties won't be able to continue paying dividends for very long.

How to Get Involved in the Stock Market on a Budget

Of course, being able to research stocks, interpret stock charts, and read stock quotes means nothing if you don't put your money where your mouth is. Many people never get involved in stock trading because they believe that they don't have enough capital to get started, but it's entirely possible to build your stock trading portfolio on a budget. It's a common misconception that you need thousands of dollars in order to open a brokerage account and start trading, but it's not true. In modernity many online brokerage firms offer brokerage accounts which have no minimums, which means you can technically open one even if you only have $10 to invest. Traditional, full service brokerage firms are more expensive and generally require that you make a minimum investment of $3,000 or more (though the required minimum investment naturally varies from brokerage firm to brokerage firm).

Those who are new to investing in the stock market are normally better off getting started by investing through a traditional brokerage firm because these kinds of firms employ professional analysts who will help them to personalize their portfolios, maximize their profits, and avoid any pitfalls. Most people don't have $3,000 lying around to open this kind of account though, which means that for many people the first step to investing in the stock market is saving up enough money to approach a traditional brokerage firm.

Luckily modern technology makes saving money easy. A lot of people struggle to save a set portion of their salary or wages every month. This has led to the development of applications which are designed specifically to help you to squirrel away your cash. Applications like Acorn, Chimes, and Qapital help investors to save up money by taking the prices of things which they purchase and rounding them up to the nearest ten. For example, if you were using one of these applications and you purchased a pair of pants for $44, the application would charge you $50, pay the pants' vendor his or her $44, and deposit $6 into your savings. Those that struggle to save (and who are thus concerned that saving up enough money to pay a traditional brokerage firm might take forever) should also consider investing their tax refund. According to the United States' Internal Revenue Service (IRS) your average American receives about $3,000 from their annual tax return, which is coincidentally just enough to cover many traditional brokerage firms' minimum investment requirements.

Realistically you need to save up about $500 before venturing into the stock market. Five hundred dollars is enough money to start investing in exchange-traded funds, treasury bonds, or in a bank's certificates of deposit

In order to help investors keep their costs even lower, some brokerage firms (like Stash) even offer investors the chance to buy fractional shares. Fractional shares are pieces of a single stock, which means that they allow you to invest $10 in Apple when buying an entire share in it would have cost you approximately $240.

It's important to keep in mind that you don't need a small fortune in order to get started, because it's vital that you don't overspend in the stock market. Due to the stock market's inherent volatility you should not invest any money in stocks that you might need back within the next five years.

Chapter 5:

Opening Your Account

By now you're likely feeling pretty well acquainted with the stock market, but you're probably still a little unsure about how exactly you should go about turning your hard-earned (and even harder-saved) money into stocks. For most middle-class Americans, the easiest way to invest in the stock market is either through their 401(k) account or their IRA. Those who do not have corporate perks like an IRA or 401(k) account or who would like to be more hands-on in their approach to stock trading are usually better off investing directly through a stockbroker and brokerage firm.

How to Use Your IRA Account to Invest in the Stock Market

Individual retirement accounts (IRAs) are accounts which investors set up in order to save for their eventual retirements. They're more than just a piggy bank for your extra pennies though, you can also use them to invest in a number of government securities and publicly-traded stocks. If you have an IRA you should consider yourself fortunate, as having one is one of the easiest ways to access the stock market. If you don't have one, don't despair — it's easy enough to open one through a bank or brokerage firm.

There are two main types of IRAs: traditional IRAs and Roth IRAs. Both traditional and Roth IRAs allow their investors to invest in anything that they see fit, from stocks, to bonds, to exchange-traded funds, and mutual funds. Anyone and everyone can open a traditional IRA. Traditional IRAs are tax deductible, which means that you can claim many of the contributions made to them back when you file for your annual tax returns. Unfortunately, income tax becomes payable on any profits made from this kind of account when it finally pays out (which means that you could lose quite a sum to tax just before retiring). Traditional IRAs are only tax deductible up to the first $6,000 that you invest in them annually (thereafter you can't claim back any further contributions through your tax return). Roth IRAs do not offer the same tax benefits because their contributions are non-deductible, however, you aren't required to pay income tax on this kind of accounts' final payout (which is why many investors opt to make use of Roth IRAs instead of traditional IRAs). Traditional IRAs are the best choice for most investors because you save money on almost every sum you choose to put away.

Fidelity, Charles Schwab, and Vanguard (three of the biggest names in the investment game) offer IRA options. Fidelity offers approximately 10,000 different types of stocks in mutual funds which their IRA holders may purchase at no additional fee — this is significant because most of the traditional brokerage firms' IRAs charge nearly $5 in trade fees per share purchased. Charles Schwab also offers free trades on Schwab funds and is world-renowned for its top stock market analysts (which means that if you choose to invest through them, you'll have the best guidance possible pertaining to long term and short term investment options). Vanguard's IRA options are even cheaper than those offered by Fidelity or Charles Schwab — in fact, Vanguard's 2016 report found that it was almost ten times cheaper than its average competitor. Vanguard's IRAs' low costs come as a result of the free trading which it offers on its exchange-traded funds and mutual funds.

Regardless of how economical Fidelity, Charles Schwab, and Vanguard might be, they're still too expensive for many investors to consider investing in. Luckily there are online options which are even cheaper. Two of the best online options are Betterment and M1 Finance. Both of these companies give their IRA investors access to highly sophisticated robo-advisors which are tasked with helping their clients craft highly personalized stock and bond portfolios. Betterment has no minimum investment requirement, which means that you can start trading through them even when money is a little tight. M1 Finance has a minimum investment requirement of $100, although it doesn't charge its investors any commissions or management fees.

If you're not looking to hand-pick all of your stocks and don't have access to a 401(k) account, an IRA may be the perfect choice for you.

How to Use Your 401(k) Account to Invest in the Stock Market

If your employer offers a retirement plan, it's probably in the form of a 401(k) account. These accounts are designed to help investors build their wealth leading up to their retirements. Employees contribute to their 401(k) accounts through monthly deductions to their paychecks. Some employers fully (or partially) match these contributions, which means that it's easy for investors' investments to double without them ever having to trade a single stock or bond.

The purpose of a 401(k) account is to allow employees to invest the money which they have contributed in an investment of their choice. This doesn't mean that 401(k) account holders have free rein, their options are generally limited to a dozen or so investments that have been handpicked by their employers (none of which are likely to be individual stocks). These investment options usually belong to mutual funds, index funds, exchange-traded funds, and target-date funds.

Just as is the case with IRAs, 401(k) accounts are also split into two distinct categories: traditional 401(k) accounts and Roth 401(k) accounts. The difference between these two types of accounts is the same as the difference between traditional IRA accounts and Roth IRA accounts. Traditional 401(k) accounts are tax deductible, which means that you can claim back contributions that you made to them in your annual tax returns —but just like traditional IRAs, their final payout is subject to income tax. Roth 401(k) accounts are not tax-deductible — but just like Roth IRAs, their final payout isn't subject to further income tax.

If you'd like to start investing in stocks through a 401(k) option offered by your employer, be sure to approach your employer's human resources department and enquire as to which investment options the company's 401(k) accounts offer.

Choosing the Right Stockbroker and Brokerage Account

A stockbroker is someone that investors pay to buy and sell stocks and bonds on their behalf. You usually 'hire' a stockbroker by enlisting the help of a full-service brokerage firm. Brokerage firms employ teams of stockbrokers, analysts, and customer service executives in order to help you access the stock market and manage your portfolio. You need to be a member of the NYSE or Nasdaq in order to be allowed to trade securities and stocks on them, which creates the need for intermediaries who are members of these stock exchanges to act on behalf of investors who are not. On top of being members of all of (or many of) the major stock exchanges, stockbrokers and brokerage firms also usually need to be registered with the Financial Industry Regulatory Authority or the Securities Investor Protection Corporations. The term 'stockbroker' is often used to refer to a brokerage firm, instead of an actual individual managing one's stocks.

There are two types of stockbrokers: full-service stockbrokers and discount stockbrokers. Full-service stockbrokers are more expensive because they do all of the research for the investor and then make individual recommendations as to which stocks would be best to invest in. Discount stockbrokers usually leave investors to their own devices and don't offer much help in terms of guidance on which stocks to invest in (although they do usually offer trading advice for an additional fee). Online discount stockbrokers have become quite popular in modernity, attracting many young investors with the promise of a chance to get rich quick. It's always tempting to go with the cheaper option, but opting to go with it can sometimes be an expensive choice. Investors who are entirely new to the stock market often need quite a bit of guidance, and are thus better off going with a full-service stockbroker despite the additional costs.

You should choose a stockbroker based off of their costs and fees, their fee structures, and their investment style.

Most stockbrokers require a minimum investment of a certain amount. Full-service stockbrokers normally require larger minimum investments, while discount stockbrokers usually require a lower minimum investment amount (if they require one at all). Margin accounts (which allow you to buy stocks and bonds on credit) usually have the highest minimum investment requirements of all.

It's also important that you enquire as to any withdrawal fees that might apply. Most stockbrokers charge an additional withdrawal fee when you choose to liquidate some of your stocks, while others won't allow you to make a withdrawal if the value of your account drops below the value of the stockbroker's required minimum investment.

Full-service stockbrokers also usually charge either an annual fee (which is normally between 1% and 1.5% of the value of all of the assets which are held within your account) or a fee for every transaction. Annual fees include inactivity fees (that you incur if your account is stagnant) and research fees. Transaction fees are charged for every transaction which takes place in your account. Most full-service stockbrokers charge approximately $150 per transaction. If you're willing to bear the financial burden, full-service stockbrokers are usually the better option. All of the big names like Charles Scwab, J.P. Morgan, and Tradestation offer full-service options.

Discount stockbrokers usually don't charge annual fees, but most of them do charge transaction fees (which range from $2 per transaction to $10 per transaction). They're the cheaper option because they don't offer nearly as much guidance as traditional stockbrokers do, which allows them to keep their costs low and thus shields their customers from additional fees. In modernity, most discount stockbrokers are online stockbrokers. Online stockbrokers and brokerage firms allow you to open an account and start trading without ever having to interact with another human being. Opening an account with an online stockbroker is quick and incredibly easy, but that doesn't mean that you should go with the first online stockbroker that comes up on Google. Some of the most popular online stockbrokers are Merrill Edge Self-Directed, TD Ameritrade, and E*Trade. Merrill Edge Self-Directed has no required minimum investment and doesn't charge any transaction fees, making it one of the cheapest options available. Merrill Edge Self-Directed is economical, but that doesn't mean that it doesn't offer trading advice and assistance to beginner investors (in fact, Merrill Edge Self-Directed is the brokerage firm to go with if you're looking for some guidance). TD Ameritrade also doesn't have a required minimum investment and doesn't charge transaction fees, but it does have one of the most user-friendly interfaces available (which makes it a good choice for those who consider themselves to be Luddites). E*Trade is just as fee-free as TD Ameritrade and Merrill Edge Self-Directed are, but it outdoes both when it comes to the sheer variety of stocks which it offers its investors. E*Trade also allows its investors to trade in mutual funds and exchange-traded funds at no cost.

It's important that you thoroughly review the fee structure of any broker or brokerage firm that you're considering employing. If a broker or brokerage firm's fees seem too good to be true, they probably are — beware of the fine print!

There are two types of stock market investors: hold investors and trade investors. Hold investors buy stocks which they believe will grow in value over the next decade or so. They generally buy stocks and hold on to them for many years before selling them and profiting from their capital appreciation. Trade investors cycle through stocks much more quickly. They buy shares which they believe are undervalued, and sell them as soon as they have reached their full potential. The stockbroker or brokerage firm that you choose to use should share your investment strategy. If you're a trade investor, you should find a stockbroker who specializes in trade investing. If you're a hold investor, you should find a stockbroker who specializes in hold investing.

If you are a trade investor and would like to try to beat the market, you should consider enlisting the services of either Fidelity or Interactive Brokers. Fidelity offers its investors access to a trading platform which it calls 'Active Trader Pro' which allows investors to buy stocks for cheaper than they would be able to anywhere else (96% of all of the stock purchases which are made through Fidelity are made at bids which are lower than the national average). Interactive Brokers offers trade investors access to a platform called 'Traders Workstation' (TWS) which is highly customizable and allows you to trade in fractional shares. Interactive

Brokers is also one of the cheapest brokerage firms around. They do not have a minimum investment requirement (so technically you could start trading with just $50 to your name) and only charge half a cent per share traded.

Deciding Whether to Make Use of a Stock-Picking Service

If you're making use of a full-service stockbroker, you don't need an additional stock advisor or stock-picking service because your stockbroker will take it upon him- or herself to research stocks and make recommendations regarding them to you. Unfortunately, full-service stockbrokers are outside of many people's financial reach, which means that investors are often left unsure of where to put their money, or when to withdraw it.

Luckily technology has been able to solve this problem to some degree, bridging the profitability gap between full-service and discount brokers. In previous years, investors looking for investment advice had to enlist the services of a stock advisor (who they went to see at his or her offices, and who charged a fee for his or her advice). In 2020, it's as easy as signing up for a robo-advisor online or making use of a stock-picking service. Robo-advisors are online platforms which make use of complex algorithms in order to measure the stock market's current performance. They then use these measurements to predict what the stock market will look like in the future — which is exactly the kind of information that investors need in order to decide whether to hold or sell their stocks. Some brokerage firms offer robo-advisory services that involve these robo-advisors running clients' accounts (buying and selling the stocks which they think are best, and selecting stocks from different sectors in order to keep their users' portfolios diversified). This might sound very futuristic, but it's actually incredibly common (many investors use robo-advisors without even realizing it). Robo-advisors have been in use for many years, and they've been proven to be an effective tool for investors looking to invest in their stocks' future capital appreciation (which means that they are not ideal for investors who would like to regularly buy and sell stocks in order to try and beat the markets). They're also a lot cheaper than opting to make use of a full-service (human) stockbroker, usually charging between 0.1% and 0.2% of the value of all of the assets in your portfolio as their annual fee. Some of the brokerage firms that make use of robo-advisors are Betterment, Ellevest, and Charles Schwab Intelligent Portfolios.

If the brokerage firm that you've chosen to make use of doesn't offer a robo-advisor, you can still enlist the services of one. It won't actively manage your account like robo-advisors do at Betterment, Ellevest, and Charles Schwab, but it will review your portfolio and give you investment advice. One of the best non-committal robo-advisors to make use of is Future Advisor. This robo-advisor's 'free' option won't buy and sell stocks on your behalf, but it will tell you which stocks it thinks you should buy, which it thinks you should sell, and when to do both. If you're feeling a bit unsure of which move to make next in the stock market, Future Advisor is a fantastic tool to use to gain some insight.

There are a number of other stock-picking services available to you if you're skeptical about using a free robo-advisor like Future Advisor. One of the best options is Warrior Trading. Warrior Trading is a company that prides itself in teaching and guiding investors. It boasts a hoard of chatrooms which investors can use to solicit advice from investment professionals and their fellow stock traders. It also offers a number of webinars, courses, and a stock market simulator (so that you can practice your fast-cycle trading skills). Warrior Trading's most attractive feature is the stock 'watchlist' (a list of stocks which their analysts believe are about to drastically increase or decrease in price) that they send out to subscribers every day.

Self-made millionaire Tim Sykes also shares his daily stock picks, for a price. Tim Sykes's subscribers receive stock market 'tips' and a stock watchlist every day for approximately $75 per month. If you choose to make use of Tim Sykes's stock-picking service, you'll also receive updates every time he makes a trade in the stock market (along with an explanation as to why he made it).

Another fantastic stock-picking option offered by a stock market millionaire is Superman Trades. For a bit less than $150 a month you'll receive Paul Scolardi's daily newsletter (containing his stock picks for the day) along with access to his blog's chat room (giving you the opportunity to direct specific questions to him and your fellow investors).

The most popular stock-picking service of 2020 is Jason Bond Picks. This service offers you access to Jason's daily watchlist and an interactive chat room filled to the brim with professionals. Jason's daily watchlists are particularly helpful because he doesn't just state what he believes a stock's price change will be, he also explains why he believes this change will occur.

First prize is still investing through a full-service stockbroker as this is where you'll receive the most support, but you certainly don't need to despair if you can't afford one. There are more than enough resources out there, like robo-advisors or stock-picking services, to help you to navigate the stock market.

Chapter 6:

How to Establish Your

Strategy and Start Investing

You now know what stocks are and what the stock market is. You know how the stock market works, which investment options are available, how to open an account, and how to choose a stockbroker. All that's left now is to apply all you've learned, and profit! Of course, a stock trader is nothing without a strategy. In fact, if you'd like to become a millionaire by trading without a strategy, you'd need to start off as a billionaire.

Trading strategies are 'rules' that you set for yourself (and follow) in order to increase your profit margins. In order to decide on a trading strategy, you need to decide how much risk you're willing to take and whether you'd like to be a long term or short term investor.

The Importance of Establishing a Stock Trading Strategy

I once heard a rich investor say that there is always money in the stock market — but whose pockets it's in changes all of the time. If you've decided to invest in the stock market, you want to make sure that it's your pocket that benefits from your participation and nobody else's. The only way you'll reliably be able to do this is if you have a watertight stock trading strategy. Without a stock trading strategy, you'd simply be buying and selling securities on a whim. A trading strategy allows you to see the 'bigger picture' and ensures that your portfolio's growth keeps heading in the right direction.

Every second Tom, Dick, and Harry will try to sell you a stock trading strategy, but it's entirely possible to develop your own if you understand the underlying principles. Your brokerage firm might also offer you certain stock trading strategies — these are certainly more reliable than the trading strategy advertisements you'll see on Facebook, but it still doesn't hurt to understand how they work and why.

There are two main kinds of stock trading strategies: fundamental stock trading strategies and technical stock trading strategies. Fundamental stock trading strategies focus on analyzing a stock's potential for profitability and growth by reviewing its holding company's financial position. They achieve this by considering the company's price-to-earnings ratio and dividends yield. Technical stock trading strategies screen stocks based on their historical performance. They do this by extrapolating data technical indicators like a stock's moving average or its relative strength index. A stock trading strategy should help you to decide when to buy stocks, when to hold on to them, and when to sell them — as well as setting realistic time frames for these purchases and sales.

You should choose a stock trading strategy based on your financial goals. You should consider how much profit you'd like to make, how much of a loss you're willing to suffer should a trade go South, and how much you'd like to earn on a trade before you'd consider selling. Most stock trading strategies set exit and entry rules in order to help you to reach these goals. An exit rule is when you tell yourself that you won't sell a stock unless its price increases to above a certain point. Setting exit rules for yourself stops you from panic selling stocks when the market experiences a downswing, possibly undermining your stocks' potential. An entry rule is when you tell yourself that you won't buy a stock unless it's selling for less than a certain price and can be considered to be undervalued. Setting entry rules for yourself helps to stop you from buying stocks on a whim, which decreases your chances of investing in a dud.

It's important that you keep a record of your trading losses and successes once you've decided on a stock trading strategy. Doing so will help you to determine whether your strategy is working. If the aforementioned record shows that you're suffering more losses than you're experiencing successes, it's time to review your stock trading strategy as you might need to consider tweaking it.

Popular Stock Trading Strategies

There are an almost unlimited amount of trading strategies available to you, but there are only a handful that have been proven to be relatively successful. You should spend some time researching some of the different stock trading strategies which have become popular in recent years before deciding on which one to employ.

The long/short equity trading strategy is based on the oldest, most fundamental law of the stock market — buy low, sell high. Traders using this strategy hold on to stocks which they believe will appreciate in value over time, while they sell the stocks in their portfolios which they anticipate will decrease in value over time. This strategy might seem like common sense to some, but many traders struggle to fully implement it. It's strongly encouraged that you earmark your shares as 'long position' or 'short position' from the get-go, so that there's never any uncertainty as to whether you should hold or sell them.

Arbitrage is one of the most well-known trading strategies out there. It involves buying stocks on one stock exchange and selling them on another for profit. An example of arbitrage would be if you bought a share in Burger King for $78 on the Nasdaq, and sold it for $80 on the NYSE. One of the major downsides to this trading strategy is that, unless your brokerage firm offers transaction fee-free transactions, small trades' profit may be lost to transaction fees (it would be counterintuitive to buy a stock in Burger King for $78, sell it for $80, and then pay $3 in transaction fees).

The next strategy is called 'pairs trading'. It involves buying two related shares in the hopes that if one decreases in value, the other will increase in value. An example of this would be investing in shares from a renewable energy company (like Enphase Energy) and an oil company (like the Murphy Energy Corporation). The reasoning behind this kind of strategy is that no matter what the market does, you profit in some way.

Forex trading is when a trader buys a sum of a certain country's currency, and then converts it to a different country's currency in order to make a profit. A forex trader might buy R19,000 of the South African Rand for $1,000 on a Tuesday, wait for a favorable election result, and sell it again for $1,100 the next day. The forex market exchange can be traded on any hour of the day from Monday to Friday, and doesn't have an 'open' or 'close' like traditional stock exchanges do. It is also far more liquid than traditional stock exchanges are, which means that you won't struggle to offload any of the investments that you've made through it.

Growth investment is a strategy which involves buying long term stocks with the sole purpose of holding on to them and selling them months or years later in order to profit from their capital appreciation. What makes this strategy a bit tricky is knowing which stocks to invest in. Not all companies increase in value over time, for instance investing in Enron as a growth investment in 1999 would have led to you losing your entire investment in 2001 after it declared bankruptcy following a fraud scandal. Blue chip stocks are usually safe growth investments, although you still need to do your homework as Enron used to be a blue chip stock too.

The opposite of growth investment is swing trading. This strategy involves investing in stocks in order to exploit their inherent volatility. Swing traders keep their ears to the ground and pay close attention to corporate gossip and newsworthy events (like droughts or forest fires). They aim to buy undervalued stocks, or stocks which they believe are about to increase in value, with the idea of holding on to them for a few weeks or months until they realize their full potential. Smart swing traders invested in shares belonging to the healthcare sector in 2019 when the Coronavirus was discovered, and were able to sell them at quite a large profit in 2020 as the value of healthcare stocks skyrocketed amidst the COVID-19 epidemic.

Day trading is a stock trading strategy which involves holding onto securities for no longer than a single trading day. Unfortunately, (or fortunately) stocks' price fluctuations over a single day are relatively small, which means that day trading is only a profitable exercise if you have enough capital to buy thousands of shares in the morning only to sell them for a profit of $0.20 per share in the evening. Just like swing traders, day traders make use of market speculation in order to predict whether a stock's price is about to increase or decrease.

Social trading (which is also known as mirror trading or mimic trading) is the stock trading strategy which is most commonly employed by those who are new to stock trading. It involves replicating the trading decisions of others and is built on the hope that the majority can't be wrong. Many brokerage firms have online platforms that sport graphs and charts which map out market trends. Day traders use these infographics to decide which stocks to invest in. It might seem like a cheap cop-out to simply copy the trading choices of others, but it's actually a fantastic learning tool. Beginner investors who engage in social trading are afforded the opportunity to see what works and what doesn't without the added stress of having to navigate a complex strategy.

You don't have to choose a specific stock trading strategy and stick to it for the rest of your life. You can switch between any number of them until you find the strategy which suits you best, or you can create a hybrid strategy by combining the characteristics and virtues of two or more previously established trading strategies. What's most important is that you find a strategy which suits your goals, budget, and lifestyle. You need to make the stock market work for you, you shouldn't be working for it.

What to Do (and What Not to Do) When Investing in the Stock Market

Hundreds (if not tens of thousands) of books have been dedicated solely to sharing stock trading tips. Every self-proclaimed stock market guru believes that he or she has found the secret to success in the stock market, but there are a few key concepts that they all seem to agree on.

Warren Buffett has often been quoted as saying that if you can't lose half of your investment in the stock market in a single day without losing a wink of sleep over it that night, you shouldn't be investing in stocks. While this might seem quite harsh to some, most financial advisors agree with him. The most important trait that a successful stock trader needs to have is the ability to leave his or her emotions at the door. Surveys have found that overtrading (which is usually caused by panic or excitement) is one of the most damaging behaviors which an investor can engage in. If you would like to be even just fractionally as successful as Warren Buffett has been, you need to learn how to make trading decisions using your head and not your heart.

Some of the world's top stock traders also encourage investors to invest in a company, and not in a stock's quote. This is because technical indicators (like moving averages) can be misleading and can make a stock appear to be a better investment than it actually is. If you base your decision to invest in a stock solely on its holding company's statistical performance, you miss out on the opportunity to research the company and to truly understand its potential for growth.

I cannot emphasize enough how important it is for those who are new to the stock market to not create debt in order to invest in it. Nothing is set in stone in the stock market, and it would be a devastating loss for your investment to go to zero and then to be left with a loan that still needs to be paid back. For this reason, beginner investors are advised to steer clear of leverage and margin accounts. While buying stocks on credit might seem like an incredibly tempting option if you believe you've discovered the next Microsoft, the consequences can be dire if the trade goes south and the stock's price plummets shortly after you've bought it.

It's also absolutely crucial that you diversify this portfolio. This means that you should not invest in stocks that all belong to the same sector. Diversification is important because stocks belonging to the same sector tend to experience similar highs and lows, which means that if you only own stocks in Microsoft and Apple and the stock market takes a dip, you'll lose money across the board and you won't have more successful stocks from other sectors to liquidate in order to rectify this loss.

Everybody knows that the first rule of the stock market is 'buy low, sell high' (which means you should buy stocks when they're in a bearish phase and sell them when they enter a bullish phase), but this doesn't mean you should allow yourself to be tempted to invest in junk stocks. If a stock has been experiencing a constant, steady decline in value over a period of time, it's not a good investment (regardless of how cheap it might be). Some stocks aren't just experiencing a bearish phase, they're failing. It might take you a while to spot the difference between the two, which is why you need to research the holding companies of the stocks that you choose to invest in (remember that publicly-traded companies have to make their financial reports available to potential investors).

If you're investing in the stock market through a stockbroker you should also avoid placing market orders (bidding on a certain stock, or requesting to liquidate stocks in your portfolio) before the stock exchange that you're planning on trading through has opened. This is because stock prices have the tendency to suddenly move upwards or downwards the minute the stock exchange opens, which means that you may end up buying stocks at a much higher price than you intended to, or you might end up selling the stocks in your portfolio for much less than you were hoping to.

A stop-loss order is your best friend if you're investing in cheap stocks in the hope that they will drastically increase in value as it mitigates the chance of you suffering a severe financial loss. Setting stop-loss orders is one of the many secrets to successful stock trading. You should consider setting one for every kind of stock you own. This kind of order tells your stockbroker or brokerage firm to sell your shares when they devalue below a certain point. For example, if you bought 100 shares in a failing company for $3 a share in the hope that the company's financial position would improve and that its shares would thus increase in value, but instead its share price drops to $0.50, you would have made a loss of $250. However, if you set a stop-loss order stating that those shares are to be sold if their price falls below $2.50 per share, it wouldn't be possible to make a loss of more than about $50.

Jacob Dayan, a co-founder of Finance Pal, believes that one of the many secrets to profiting on the stock market is to invest in an array of stocks that range from being low-risk to being high risk. The majority of stock advisors seem to agree. While there's some debate on the ideal ratio, your portfolio should consist of about 70% low-risk stocks (these are usually stocks that belong to blue chip companies), 20% moderate risk stocks, and 10% high-risk stocks. Low-risk stocks do not offer the kind of capital appreciation that well-picked moderate and high-risk stocks do, but you're usually relatively assured of the fact that they won't lose most of their value overnight and many of them offer attractive dividend policies. Moderate and high-risk stocks may lose most of their value in the blink of an eye, but they're also normally cheaper to acquire than low-risk stocks, which means that investors are able to sell them for much more significant profits when they do undergo capital appreciation. Some of the best low-risk stocks to invest in belong to Hormel, VEREIT, and Enterprise Products Partners. All three of these companies regularly pay out dividends to their investors (which means that they offer a regular source of income to investors) and have proven that they can survive everything from management scandals to recessions (which means that you can assume that they won't be going anywhere anytime soon). The Scientific Games Corporation and Splunk are moderate risk stocks that have shown increased growth and profitability over the past three years. Examples of high-risk stocks are Teva Pharmaceutical, Chesapeake Energy, and Canadian Solar. These stocks have all suffered significant losses over the past couple of years, which means that their stock prices are low, however, these companies have all made promising moves towards bettering their prospects which means that there's a chance that their stock prices may exponentially increase in value over the next couple of years.

Few people realize that there are also ideal times to trade in the stock market. You should try to avoid buying any new stocks before lunch, because corporate reports and government statistics which might drastically drive their prices up or down are released in the morning. If you're looking to sell some of the stocks in your portfolio, you should consider doing so on the first two or last two days of the month. This is because stock prices tend to increase over this time period as the demand from investors who have just received their monthly salaries skyrockets (which means you'll be able to sell your stocks for more than you'd be able to get for them in the middle of the month). Inversely, if you'd like to buy stocks you should consider doing so somewhere between the tenth and the twenty-second of the month because this is when investors' enthusiasm starts to wane, the demand decreases, and consequently stock prices decline.

There's no recipe to become a stock market millionaire. Your stock trading success will depend entirely upon your own determination, grit, and willingness to learn. Don't get discouraged if you lose money on a few trades at first, it will take a while before you get into the swing of things.

Conclusion

You may have started reading this book as someone that was unsure of how the stock market worked, but by the end of chapter six, you should have learned how to invest, why to invest, and where to invest — which means that you now know everything you need to know in order to get started.

I hope that there's no doubt left in your mind that you're capable of succeeding in the stock market and growing your personal wealth. Opening a brokerage account and getting started is so easy. There's nothing to it. Stock trading is not particularly complicated, you don't need to know how to do calculus or algebra, you don't need a degree in finance or economics — all you need is the courage to start. In fact, I dare you to open your browser and to contact some of the brokerage firms mentioned in this book as soon as you're done reading this page. You could open your own personal brokerage account within the next hour or two if you act swiftly.

Don't be tempted to start making excuses as to why you can't start investing today. If you have $100 to your name and the willingness to try, there's absolutely nothing stopping you. You won't become the next George Soros (or be able to fund your next holiday) by pensively considering investing in the stock market — you actually need to do it.

Why don't you leave a review on this book detailing which stocks you're planning to invest in and which investment strategy you're planning to make use of once you're done contacting a brokerage firm? That way you have an internet memorial to look back on in ten years' time when your wealth has increased tenfold. Leaving us a review helps us to spread the good news — that absolutely anyone can better their financial position by investing in the stock market.

References

11 Best Online Brokers for Stock Trading of March 2020. NerdWallet. (2020). Retrieved 24 March 2020, from <https://www.nerdwallet.com/best/investing/online-brokers-for-stock-trading>.

4 Ways to Predict Market Performance. Investopedia. (2020). Retrieved 24 March 2020, from <https://www.investopedia.com/articles/07/mean_reversion_martingale.asp>.

6 Things You Should Know Before Opening An Investment Account. Business Insider. (2020). Retrieved 25 March 2020, from <https://www.businessinsider.com/things-to-know-before-opening-investment-account-2018-12>.

9 Most Important Functions of Stock Exchange/Secondary Market. Your Article Library. (2020). Retrieved 24 March 2020, from <http://www.yourarticlelibrary.com/economics/market/9-most-important-functions-of-stock-exchangesecondary-market/8766>.

An Overview of Bull and Bear Markets. Investopedia. (2020). Retrieved 26 March 2020, from

<https://www.investopedia.com/insights/diggi
ng-deeper-bull-and-bear-markets/>.

Best Investment Accounts For Young Investors.
Money Under 30. (2020). Retrieved 25 March
2020, from
<https://www.moneyunder30.com/best-
investment-accounts>.

Biggest Stock Market Crashes in History. TheStreet.
(2020). Retrieved 25 March 2020, from
<https://www.thestreet.com/markets/history-
of-stock-market-crashes-14702941>.

Buffett, W., & Andrews, D. (2012). The Oracle Speaks
(pp. 35 - 70). B2 Books.

Chokkavelu, A. (2020). 20 of the Top Stocks to Buy in
2020 (Including the 2 Every Investor Should
Own). The Motley Fool. Retrieved 25 March
2020, from
<https://www.fool.com/investing/top-stocks-
to-buy.aspx>.

Collins, G. (2020). Stock Market Forecast 2020 - 2021 -
Corona Virus Stock Market Crash Correction
Dow NASDAQ S&P. Gord Collins. Retrieved
24 March 2020, from
<https://gordcollins.com/stock-
market/factors-forecast/>.

Dow Jones - DJIA - 100 Year Historical Chart.
Macrotrends. (2020). Retrieved 25 March 2020,

from
<https://www.macrotrends.net/1319/dow-jones-100-year-historical-chart>.

Farrington, R. (2020). What Type of Investment Account Do I Open?. The College Investor. Retrieved 25 March 2020, from <https://thecollegeinvestor.com/1330/type-investment-account-open/>.

Friedrich, J. (2020). *The Stock Market and the Economy – How do they impact each other? – Altavista Wealth Management.* Altavistawealth.com. Retrieved 24 March 2020, from <https://altavistawealth.com/stock-market-and-the-economy/>.

Goldberg, M. (2020). *Brokerage Checking Accounts - Pros and Cons.* Bankrate. Retrieved 24 March 2020, from <https://www.bankrate.com/banking/checking/pros-cons-of-brokerage-checking-accounts/>.

Guide to the Markets. J.P. Morgan Asset Management. (2020). Retrieved 24 March 2020, from <https://am.jpmorgan.com/us/en/asset-management/gim/adv/insights/guide-to-the-markets>.

How the Stock Market Was Started & by Whom. Smallbusiness.chron.com. (2020). Retrieved 24 March 2020, from

<https://smallbusiness.chron.com/stock-market-started-whom-14745.html>.

How to Build a Successful Budget Plan That Works. Investor Junkie. (2020). Retrieved 24 March 2020, from <https://investorjunkie.com/personal-finance/build-budget/>.

How to Buy a Stock. WSJ Guides. (2020). Retrieved 24 March 2020, from <https://guides.wsj.com/personal-finance/investing/how-to-buy-a-stock/>

How to Choose an Online Stock Broker. Investopedia. (2020). Retrieved 25 March 2020, from <https://www.investopedia.com/investing/complete-guide-choosing-online-stock-broker/>.

How to Invest in Stocks: A Step-by-Step for Beginners. NerdWallet. (2020). Retrieved 24 March 2020, from <https://www.nerdwallet.com/blog/investing/how-to-invest-in-stocks/>.

How to Invest in the Stock Market. The Balance. (2020). Retrieved 24 March 2020, from <https://www.thebalance.com/how-do-individual-investors-buy-stocks-3306180>.

How To Invest On A Shoestring Budget. Investopedia. (2020). Retrieved 24 March 2020, from <https://www.investopedia.com/articles/younginvestors/07/shoestring_budget.asp>.

How to Open a Brokerage Account: A Step-by-Step Guide. The Ascent. (2020). Retrieved 24 March 2020, from <https://www.fool.com/the-ascent/buying-stocks/articles/how-to-open-a-brokerage-account-a-step-by-step-guide/>.

How to Pick a Broker. Investopedia. (2020). Retrieved 25 March 2020, from <https://www.investopedia.com/articles/younginvestors/06/firstbroker.asp>.

How to Read a Stock Table. For Dummies. (2020). Retrieved 24 March 2020, from <https://www.dummies.com/personal-finance/investing/how-to-read-a-stock-table/>.

Hur, J. (2020). History of The Stock Market. BeBusinessed. Retrieved 25 March 2020, from <https://bebusinessed.com/history/history-of-the-stock-market/>.

Jackson, A. (2020). *Stock Market Guide: What Is the Stock Market and How Does it Work?*. NerdWallet. Retrieved 24 March 2020, from <https://www.nerdwallet.com/blog/investing/what-is-the-stock-market/>.

Lam, J. (2020). *Stock Market 101: What Is the Stock Market and How Does It Work?* Quicken Loans. Retrieved 24 March 2020, from <https://www.quickenloans.com/blog/stock-market-101-stock-market-work>.

Must know: Difference between Investing and Trading. Outlook India. (2020). Retrieved 24 March 2020, from <https://www.outlookindia.com/outlookmoney/fixed-assets/must-know-difference-between-investing-and-trading-2197>.

Patton, M. (2020). Five Basics You Should Definitely Know About The Stock Market. Forbes. Retrieved 25 March 2020, from <https://www.forbes.com/sites/mikepatton/2015/04/28/five-basics-you-should-definitely-know-about-the-stock-market/>.

Premarket Stock Trading. Cnn.com. (2020). Retrieved 24 March 2020, from <https://www.cnn.com/business/markets/premarkets/>.

Purpose of the Stock Market. Pocketsense. (2020). Retrieved 24 March 2020, from <https://pocketsense.com/purpose-stock-market-1350.html>.

Rossolillo, N. (2020). *5 Bold Predictions for the 2020 Stock Market.* The Motley Fool. Retrieved 24 March 2020, from <https://www.fool.com/investing/2019/12/29/5-bold-predictions-for-the-2020-stock-market.aspx>.

Stock Market Data - Dow Jones, Nasdaq, S&P 500. Money.cnn.com. (2020). Retrieved 24 March

2020,   from
<http://money.cnn.com/data/markets/>.

Stock Market Rich Stories (Traders and Investors Who
       Got Rich). The Robust Trader. (2020).
       Retrieved   24   March   2020,   from
       <https://therobusttrader.com/stock-market-
       rich-stories/>.

Technical Analysis of Stocks with Candlesticks.
       Americanbulls. (2020). Retrieved 26 March
       2020,   from
       <https://www.americanbulls.com/Default.aspx
       ?lang=en>.

The Birth of Stock Exchanges. Investopedia. (2020).
       Retrieved   24   March   2020,   from
       <https://www.investopedia.com/articles/07/st
       ock-exchange-history.asp>.

The Birth of Stock Exchanges. Investopedia. (2020).
       Retrieved   24   March   2020,   from
       <https://www.investopedia.com/articles/07/st
       ock-exchange-history.asp>.

The History of 'Bull' and 'Bear' Markets. Merriam-
       Webster. (2020). Retrieved 26 March 2020,
       from   <https://www.merriam-
       webster.com/words-at-play/the-origins-of-the-
       bear-and-bull-in-the-stock-market>.

The Importance Of Diversification. Investopedia.
       (2020). Retrieved 24 March 2020, from

<https://www.investopedia.com/investing/im
portance-diversification/>.

The Role of the Stock Exchange in the Economy. Finance.
(2020). Retrieved 24 March 2020, from
<https://finance.zacks.com/role-stock-
exchange-economy-5026.html>.

The Ultimate Guide to Stock Market APIs for 2020.
Medium. (2020). Retrieved 24 March 2020,
from <https://towardsdatascience.com/the-
ultimate-guide-to-stock-market-apis-for-2020-
1de6f55adbb>.

The Ultimate Guide to Stock Market APIs for 2020.
Medium. (2020). Retrieved 24 March 2020,
from <https://towardsdatascience.com/the-
ultimate-guide-to-stock-market-apis-for-2020-
1de6f55adbb>.

Trading Terms You Need to Know. Timothysykes.com.
(2020). Retrieved 24 March 2020, from
<https://www.timothysykes.com/blog/trading
-terms-you-need-to-know/>.

Understanding a Candlestick Chart. Investopedia. (2020).
Retrieved 24 March 2020, from
<https://www.investopedia.com/trading/candl
estick-charting-what-is-it/>.

What Causes Stock Prices to Change? | Desjardins
Online Brokerage. Disnat.com. (2020).
Retrieved 24 March 2020, from

<https://www.disnat.com/en/learning/trading
-basics/stock-basics/what-causes-stock-prices-
to-change>.

What Is a Brokerage Account and How Do I Open
One?. NerdWallet. (2020). Retrieved 24 March
2020, from
<https://www.nerdwallet.com/article/investin
g/what-is-how-to-open-brokerage-account>.

Why Do Companies Sell Stocks. Sapling. (2020). Retrieved
24 March 2020, from
<https://www.sapling.com/5149719/do-
companies-sell-stocks>.

Worst Stock Market Crash in U.S. History. The Balance.
(2020). Retrieved 24 March 2020, from
<https://www.thebalance.com/stock-market-
crash-of-1929-causes-effects-and-facts-
3305891>.

Yochim, D. (2020). How to Research Stocks: 4 Steps
for Beginners. NerdWallet. Retrieved 24 March
2020, from
<https://www.nerdwallet.com/blog/investing/
how-to-research-stocks/>.